ART BUSINESS TODAY

HANDBOOKS IN INTERNATIONAL ART BUSINESS

Series Editor: Iain Robertson
Advisory Editors: Jeffrey Boloten and Jos Hackforth-Jones

The art market is now a multi-billion-dollar industry employing hundreds of thousands of professionals worldwide. Working within the art market brings a specific set of challenges, which are distinct from those of the conventional business world. Aimed at art world professionals and those working within the many sectors of art business, as well as those preparing for careers in the commercial art world, the Handbooks in International Art Business provide a series of authoritative reference guides to the structure and working of the international art market, incorporating core topics such as Art Law and Ethics as well as guides to different market sectors.

The Handbooks are written by experts in their field, many of whom teach at, or are graduates of, the MA in Art Business at Sotheby's Institute of Art. Sotheby's Institute of Art has pioneered the field of art business as both a professional and an academic discipline. Its MA in Art Business was established in 1998.

ART BUSINESS TODAY

20 KEY TOPICS

Edited by Jos Hackforth-Jones and Iain Robertson

Lund Humphries
in association with Sotheby's Institute of Art

CONTENTS

ART AND LAW

BUYING AND SELLING

DEALERS AND COLLECTORS

ACKNOWLEDGEMENTS

These writings about art business owe much to the history and heritage of the field at Sotheby's Institute of Art–London (SIA–L) and to its many inspirational teachers and students. The MA in Art Business at SIA–L has been in the vanguard of this discipline and was first launched by the late Vivian Flaxman in 1998. Since then, hundreds of students have grappled with the topics addressed in this text and this book is a tribute both to them and to their teachers.

Art Business Today was conceived over a relatively long time frame but written in a remarkably short period. We thank Derrick Chong who, with Iain Robertson, was responsible for the initial proposal. Both editors are enormously grateful to our contributors for the quality of their essays, prompt compliance with deadlines, quick turnaround and continued good humour.

A number of other colleagues at SIA–L have contributed to this publication. We are indebted to our Librarian, Heidi Rasmussen, for her wonderful responsiveness, advice and assistance. Jo Foy's expertise in Corporate Social Responsibility has enhanced the text and her formidable management and organisational skills have been invaluable. Both editors are appreciative of her continued enthusiasm and dedication to this project. Jonathan Woolfson, Deputy Director at SIA–L kindly read an early draft of the Introduction and his comments and insights enabled us to whip it into better shape. Any lapses or mistakes are, of course, our own. Sim Hackforth-Jones's expertise in globalisation was a useful reference point. Warm thanks are also due to Charles Hill, Sarah James and Anneke Irving.

Colleagues at Lund Humphries are a joy to work with and we thank Lucy Myers for her patience and direction. Sarah Thorowgood's management has ensured that the project ran smoothly. Anjali Bulley's editing has been impressive, kept us up to the mark and enhanced the text.

Jos Hackforth-Jones and Iain Robertson

PREFACE

This is the fifth book in a series of specialist handbooks that foregrounds the study of art business. In many ways, as the title makes evident, this volume of the five adheres most faithfully to the subject. Art business today is a multi-disciplinary topic that encounters the legal, technological, philosophical, connoisseurial, economic and political aspects of the art world. The art market and the art world are consequences of actions that affect society at large. The collecting of works of art, which was once an entrenched elite's avocation, has become a democratic, open market-place for an often uninitiated minority that enjoys unprecedented amounts of wealth.

The price of art, which was once protected from the wider commodity market, is now susceptible to the instantaneous change in the fortune of stocks, shares and bullion. The art market mechanism, which evolved out of the state's patrimony into one arrogated by a handful of Western European, bourgeois intermediaries, has now been claimed by those with significant surplus wealth to expend. Technology has made access to art easier for a greater number of people with a willingness to spend money.

The laws and ethical codes that have had to measure up to the transmogrification of the market and its world are at times strained. Decisions that were once made at the nod of a head or with a handshake, are now made at the click of switch. Antiquities that were formerly sold with impunity and acquired by great European and American museums are now subject to stringent controls and redress. The consequence of buying or selling an illicit work of art is egregious.

This book seeks to unpack many of these complex and fascinating themes.

Iain Robertson and Jos Hackforth-Jones

INTRODUCTION

Art Business Today engages with the discipline and related professional practices of art business. Art business is interpreted as that crucial space defined by the intersection of the art world with the art market. While the focus begins with the art, together with the concomitant activities of evaluation, contextualisation and appraisal, these texts discuss the discipline and related professional practices of art business via the examination of selling, distribution and the consumption of art together with legal and ethical considerations. In recent years there have been numerous texts exploring both the art world and the art market, but very few that introduce the reader to all aspects of the art business.

Since the turn of the millennium, and following the dramatic shift in the scale and scope of the art market, many publications have sought to consider the impact of this phenomenon on both the art world and the art market – particularly the unparalleled expansion of the contemporary art market.

The growth of art market studies as an academic field and, more particularly of art business as an academic discipline predominantly based in the social sciences alongside cultural and visual art studies, has witnessed a corresponding increase in academic articles, books and conferences. Since 2000 numerous academic articles have considered the economics of the art market. These papers can be found in, for example, the *Journal of Cultural Economics*, *Poetics*, the *International Journal of Cultural Management*, the *International Journal of Cultural Heritage and Management*, the *Journal of Financial and Quantitative Analysis*, the *American Economic Review*, the *European Economic Review* and the *Harvard Business Review*. The fact that the last four prestigious academic journals are concerned primarily with issues beyond the field of the arts or culture, but now include art and commerce amongst their subjects, is symptomatic of the expansion of our field of investigation.

This collection of essays adopts a broad approach to art business and explores not only the transactional marketplace with its emphasis on buying, selling, collecting and investment, but also the increasingly porous boundaries across the public and private sectors. We also consider the dynamics behind different market sectors and the more recent importance of emerging markets as well as the processes behind some of these developments – such as globalisation, ethics and public funding. Another distinctive feature is the examination of key legal and ethical issues intertwined with a focus on the object. Thus, in the art business ecosystem due diligence in the transactional process requires an understanding of connoisseurship, conservation, processes of authentication and related issues such as art theft, fakes and forgeries. The main thrust of our narrative is focused on the West where the marketplace is most developed. However we also look at other key regions such as the Middle East, South America and Asia, all of whose art ecosystems are evolving rapidly.

In recent years there has been an increasing focus in the Academy (by which we mean in this context tertiary institutions of learning and cultural institutions such as museums) on what we have defined above as art business, but there continue to be very few university degrees that engage with the field as a discrete unit and as a branch of the social sciences – the exceptions are Sotheby's Institute of Art (with an MA in Art Business established in 1998), Christie's Education with an MSc in Art, Law and Business established in 2013 and masters programmes at the International Studies in History and Business of Art (IESA) and the University of Zurich. Increasing numbers of universities run courses that include some art market studies but these tend to be grafted on to a degree in Arts Administration, Arts Management or Business Studies or attached to an MBA – a cut-and-paste approach which does not always fully appreciate that the roots of art business are in the business of art with all its complexities and contradictions, rather than in the art of business.

Since 2010 the acceleration of interest in the study of art business has been evident in both the professional art world and the Academy. This interest is perhaps best reflected in the emergence of the Art Business conference held in London since 2014, but scheduled in 2017 for other major global centres such as New York. This conference focuses on issues ranging from insurance to tax and law. Since 2015 the rising number of conferences exploring the history and current state of the art market, collecting, connoisseurship, the dealers and museums, the collector-dealer relationship, authentication, art and cultural heritage, the gift and its legacy and collecting – have all attracted an international audience of practitioners and experts. The choice of key topics in this text reflects this international growth in the discipline of art business.

From the 1950s to the 1970s, the art market developed out of a series of national markets into a transatlantic one, starting from when Sotheby's purchased the US auction house Parke-Bernet in 1964. The French art market could be described as an international art entrepôt (as significant as the Anglo-American alliance) until the late 1970s. By the 1980s the art market had grown into a transnational one. Dealers and collectors from all over the world were now active participants in premier auctions taking place in the spring and the autumn.

The expansion of the market into a truly global trade rose out of the ashes of the financial crash of 1991. By the millennium, the art market had grown to include much of East Asia, parts of the Middle East, India and China. It should be explained that the spread of the market took place in dissimilar components in each territory throughout the period of inflation. So, the international auction market thrived in the Middle East; the alpha Western dealerships profited from East Asia, while national operators from the plethora of smaller emerging markets sought to join the legion of most highly regarded galleries representing the work of cutting-edge contemporary artists at globally branded art fairs. The systemic problems of an underdeveloped cultural infrastructure were addressed by East Asia first. An institutional development programme was started in South Korea shortly after the World Cup in that country in 2002. Taiwan had begun its museum-building programme in the 1990s, perhaps the first emerging market territory to do so. Qatar, Abu Dhabi and the city of Shanghai, in particular, devised blueprints for the twenty-first-century art world omphalos.

Today the Internet has, theoretically, enabled more territories to participate in an art fest. But the online vehicles that provide sales platforms and information sources, and as a result make the market more transparent and accessible, have hit obstacles from other overarching ecosystems. In a similar way, product differentiation exemplified in the new and specialist sub-sectors of photography and twentieth-century and contemporary design is subject to seismic compulsions outside the art world.

Nationalism, censorship, anti-globalism and cultural protectionism have all conspired to undermine the greater whole that seemed so assured a decade ago. The forces of cultural autonomy or at least distinctiveness in South America, represented by the term *Indigenismo*, Asian Nativism and Sino-Russian nationalism are today massed against globalism and economic liberalism. The art market is buffeted by both tidal waves and its future will be decided by the outcome of this wider cultural struggle. One thought is that the international market will fragment into regions, within which conduct will observe local customs, becoming autarkic and distinct from any accepted norm. There may no longer be an accepted norm. The ineffectiveness of international protocols for the 'actual' protection of cultural property has already emboldened domestic markets to seek ever greater degrees of autonomy. The detachment of the regions will be characterised by transnational relationships between competing brands from emerging and core markets; in short glocalism.

It is no longer a surprise to see emerging market brands associated with global sporting events, where once the fascia boards surrounding pitches and courts were emblazoned only with familiar Western logos and company names. In the art market, Sotheby's and Christie's are now challenged in Asia by the Chinese State auction house, Poly (Baoli), and its commercial equivalent, China Guardian. This is the tip of the competition the former duopoly faces. Specialist auction houses such as Russian-owned Phillips and regional operators such as Lasarati in Indonesia, Taiwan-based Ravenel and the American internet auction house Heritage are all targeting the blue-chip companies' traditional hunting grounds.

Dealers from emerging markets, most of whom have been hitherto excluded from the global art fairs, are reasserting themselves in local markets and patronising national and regional fairs. The net worth of East Asia is equivalent to that of Western Europe or the United States and it is growing at a rate far greater than its two rivals. In emerging markets cultural infrastructure projects are funded by sovereign wealth rather than external investment and debt, which is a feature of Western development. Asia in particular is a mix of predominantly private capital and state approval. With the validation of national institutions comes cultural confidence. The detached economic and cultural model pioneered in Western Europe for over a century, one in which the public good is paid for by government and the market is disqualified from art theory and history, seems redundant. The holes sprung in the system are now plugged by private sponsorship and influence. The declaration of cultural authority asserted by public servants now appears out of step with relativist market prerogatives motivated by taste, fashion and price.

We must conclude that the stentorian cries of pragmatic art market traders have pierced the ears of quixotic curators. Western European governments no longer have the funds or political will to prop up culture for its own sake. The second White Paper on the Arts published in 2016 by the UK government promotes greater inclusivity than its 1965 predecessor but does not propose to spend on culture. In Britain as in much of the West, there will be much less government in culture in the future. The situation is different in Asia, particularly in China and also in the Middle East and Russia, where one could argue government still has a strong influence on cultural style, production and content.

Much art world practice relating to the making of art continues to take for granted that art is different and few would find this a contentious view. Art cannot be traded like any other physical commodity. Most dealers and auction houses continue to publicly insist that they do not sell art for its potential as an investment, but for the joy and pleasure and possibly the status that ownership of a beautiful object will bring. Any increase in material value is, for the greater part, seen as a bonus. Today it is difficult to distinguish the idea of an art world from that of an art market, but in this volume we hope that we have achieved that.

More recently the processes of globalisation that have affected all aspects of the art world should mean that national and local markets can no longer rely on shared understandings and informal codes of practice at home as increasing numbers of outsiders compete for the benefits of a larger and wider market. Ultimately this has resulted in a movement 'toward a more clearly defined set of rules to cover duties and expectations in a multinational marketplace' which has inevitably had legal and ethical ramifications. Indeed the long-held perception that the art market is opaque and lacks regulation is shown here to no longer be true. Together with the accessibility and expansion of information via the internet, this has also encouraged transparency. Whether there should be more transparency and regulation is a live issue, with many in both the public and private sectors fearing that the invention and application of further national and international laws and regulations will prove to be an antinome, with one law contradicting the other.

One theme that emerges in many of the essays in this book, and which is an international and transnational phenomenon, is the porousness of divisions between public and private art sectors – particularly in Europe, with the public sector appropriating from the private in order to remain viable and be less dependent on government subvention. Thus a public institution such as a museum may include fundraising and sponsorship at its core as well as running businesses such as shops, restaurants and licensing and publishing divisions. Increasingly commercial institutions such as dealerships, galleries and auction houses seek to incorporate practices associated with the public sector for reputational gain. Examples include the catalogue, exhibitions of works on loan and those that are not for sale as well as references to works of art as being of 'museum quality'. Substantial changes here are also reflective of the change in the 'institutional ecology of art'.[1]

Derrick Chong goes further in his essay on 'Public Funding and the Art Market' when he acknowledges the importance of museums to the art ecosystem. He suggests that the nature of museum funding reflects the ideology of respective national governments. He asserts that there are wider benefits to public subsidy for the arts that extend beyond our art world into society. This public good might be thought to intersect with the art world, even to be a part of it. However, this is not the case. The art world serves the art market and any external 'benefits' that accrue outside this relationship are distinct and separate. That is why in Europe museums and galleries are paid, as Chong explains, partly out of taxes and by direct government subvention. Governments in Europe are morally obliged to shoulder the burden of social need in order to enhance societal cohesion. A great part of this need is represented by education and recreation, two endeavours to which art contributes. While the art world and its market are notionally a part of society, the privacy and exclusiveness upon which they thrive often draw them apart from the rest of society.

The situation is different in the United States, where nearly all the great cultural institutions are funded by private means. Worldwide there has been a spurt in the growth of private museum building in recent years, particularly in emerging countries – most notably China. Melanie Gerlis suggests that nearly all this construction has at its root money, whether that be investment, tax efficiency or philanthropy (see 'Private Museums and the Art Market'). Visitor numbers are generally extremely low for the vast majority of these institutions. In both emerging countries and the West, the division between private patronage and public duty is increasingly occluded. A case in point is the 2012 retrospective of the work of Damien Hirst (b.1964) at London's Tate Modern. It was underwritten by the Qatar Museums Authority, which owns a number of works by the artist. The Tate exhibition undoubtedly added to the symbolic value of its collection. The defining characteristic that the private museum owners share, Gerlis explains, is the membership of a club of like-minded individuals. Other writers, notably Olav Velthuis in his book *Talking Prices* (2005), have been at pains to emphasise how significant 'symbolic' value garnered from the art world is to the art market, and this notion is a persistent thought shared by many of the writers in this volume. A perhaps more practical observation to be made of the private museum club is its similarity to the group of preferred clients assembled by senior auction houses and the most prestigious art galleries. These last two groups inhabit the art market and are a critical part of the art business ecosystem but are also to be found in the liminal zone of private museum owners.

The art market has a remarkable characteristic in that nearly all of its millions of commodities are unique. It is, in economic parlance, a market that deals in heterogeneous products. David Bellingham in his entry 'Art Market Sectors' writes of the need to rationalise this statistical conundrum through the categorisation of art market sectors and sub-sectors.[2] Bellingham raises the crucial origin of this phenomenon. In the last three centuries BC, he explains, the Romano-Hellenistic art market developed simultaneously with art history. However the art historical discourse of the early Greco-Roman world privileged the 'fine art' of painting and sculpture over precious metal decorative art objects which were deemed equivalent in value by the market.

There are other insistent words of classification that the writers use throughout the book. For instance, the art market is divided into three sectors. This separation derives from an article written in the *Journal of Cultural Economics* in 1994.[3] In it the authors write of the primary dealer market, those intermediaries who are responsible for showing and developing the art and careers of living artists, some of whom have recently graduated from art school. They describe the secondary market as the resale dealer market. The tertiary market is the auction house market. There are other terms involving the treatment and use of art as a financial instrument. The lexicon of financial and art terms begins with a comparison of gilts to high-quality Old Master paintings, the best modern and the highest-quality Asian art and antiques. The financial term 'blue chip security' is applied to the highest-value contemporary and post-war art. Index-linked bonds and futures are practical financial terms for early stage (primary) art. Junk bonds refer to art that may have significant aggregate but no unit resale value. 'Art as Investment' addresses the incapacity of investment-grade art to produce a dividend as well as examining how art may become a financial commodity and also be securitised.

Frenetic buying in the market for contemporary Chinese art in the 1990s has turned the contemporary art market paradigm on its head. In this instance, comparably high prices were paid (and are still being paid) for the work of young Chinese oil painters who did not receive significant validation from the art world or support, until a late stage, from international dealers and collectors. It appears that the work of these artists has endured at least as long, if not longer, than much validated contemporary art backed by the West's alpha dealers.

Globalisation is a concept that this book has been obliged to address. From the early formation of large urban civilisations, to the discovery of new worlds through oceangoing travel, to the stimulation of capitalism, the twentieth century has seen a massively accelerated spread and mix of peoples and cultures around the world. The last 25 years have seen a revolutionary explosion in technology, faster communication and travel combined with an increase in major conurbations. The future is uncertain but an insistent tension between innate local interests and broad global aspirations appears to be tightening. Furthermore, a transference of economic and political power is taking place today. Its trajectory is away from Europe and towards China, Russia and the myriad resource-rich states of Central Asia and the Persianate world, although this view is not universally shared. In *The Smartest Places on Earth: Why Rustbelts are the Emerging Hotspots of Global Innovation* (2016) by Antoine van Agtmael (the inventor of the term emerging markets) and Fred Bakker, it is argued that the Western world's rustbelts (cities, such as Detroit, adversely affected by de-industrialisation) are the new sources of innovation; the new brain-belts. It is a persuasive idea with a lot of substance, but it is predicated on the notion that the workforce in liberal democracies is the best equipped in the world to innovate and to work collaboratively. It is based clearly on very recent developments before the dust, so to speak, has been allowed to settle, and it ignores similar things occurring in China's own rustbelt in succeeding years and indeed the economic and intellectual potential in the multitude of conurbations in India and South America.

It should be emphasised that China's investment across a great range of industry in the United States is escalating. China's investment in the US accounts for perhaps 10 per cent of its total foreign investment, much of which is now spearheaded by small and medium-sized enterprises (SMEs). Since 2008, that country has accelerated its acquisitions of 'distressed' assets in Europe and the United States and reduced its exposure to Africa and even Asia. The ultimate success of the brain-belt is surely reliant on the indefinite stay and intellectual contribution of a great army of non-Western, elite graduates who are now prominent in the West's top-tier educational institutions. It has become clear then, that in relation to business practice, whether in reference to the innovative capacity of the West's rustbelt or the resurrection of emerging markets, the term globalisation is both highly complex and multivalent. The economic fragility of globalisation extends to the difficulties inherent in the notion of a universal and homogenised culture. From whichever source the next economic revolution comes forth, it may be that many forms of production and consumption will be local or even glocal rather than global.

This moves our debate on to the transmogrification of the art market and art world. Some of this change has been wrought by technology discussed by Marios Samdanis. Today empowered tech entrepreneurs are directly linking sellers to buyers, thus bypassing the gatekeepers. This is a direct threat, the writer continues, to the 'perceived significance of a work of art' known throughout as symbolic value. It has also meant that emerging markets are able to promote local artists and directly connect with foreign sellers. So, perhaps the market spike in unvalidated contemporary Chinese oil paintings in the 1990s through to 2005 was a prelude to the market's evolution. Technology, in short, purports to supplant the role of an actual intermediary. It is probably less successful in so doing than its protagonists would have us believe, but there is evidence that the Generation Y are more likely to buy online than seasoned collectors. The impact of the participation of the wider society in the art market has yet to be felt in full, but an indication of its eventual effect can be seen in the high number of branded editions produced by artists like Takashi Murakami (b.1962) under his KaiKai Kiki label. Such market expansion has been assisted greatly by technology. Samdanis observes that new dependencies are formed between the technological platforms and the established art world, which certainly complicates the picture. What does appear clear is that wholesale access to art is not accompanied by heightened consumer sensitivities, intellectual ambition or spiritual enlightenment. Rather it may be the simple victory of the noisy consumer. The triumph of consumption is particularly acute, as Samdanis points out, in 'apps' used as digital museum guides and displays, which at best enhance and enlighten the experience for the visitor and make exhibitions more accessible. At worst they serve to distance the audience still further from the work of art, reducing the museum visit to a window-shopping escapade, full of calibrated excitement.

In recent years there have been a number of sectors of significant interest in the market, including art from emerging countries, contemporary photography and Design Art. Design Art offers an illuminating example of how a new area inserts itself into the art market. The boundaries between art and design are permeable, as designers experiment with materials and form. This has opened up new market possibilities. Contemporary art auctions now include contemporary artefacts by well-known designers and one result of this has been the emergence of new art fairs specialising in this phenomenon such as DesignArt London in 2007, renamed the Pavilion of Art and

Design (PAD) in 2009. Typically in this new genre, form follows idea rather than function. Contemporary collectors are prepared to pay a premium for works that not only furnish their houses but also complement their fine art collecting.

Ethics lie at the core of our understanding of and interaction with art. The discussion of ethics, with its philosophical and moral underpinning and legal implications, also engages with many of the other essays, including 'Authenticity', 'Fakes, Forgeries and Thefts', 'The Auction Process', 'Due Diligence' and 'Rights of Artists'. This reminds us that while the art world is perceived by some to be under-regulated, it relies on its stakeholders to behave in a principled fashion, so that for centuries art transactions have frequently relied on 'gentlemen's agreements'. Furthermore, as David Bellingham and Tom Christopherson explain, this pervasive lack of transparency together with the absence of a particular legal framework for art business has meant that there was a frequently unspoken and even unconscious premise that the art world 'was governed by laws and ethical codes which were different from run-of-the-mill commercial transactions and relationships'. This resulted in players setting their own boundaries and frameworks. That said, over the last half century there has been a marked international shift in relation to the acquisition and movement of items of cultural heritage that can be traced back to the 1954 Convention for the Protection of Cultural Property in the Event of Armed Conflict. Later UNESCO conventions in the 1970s relate to the export, transfer of ownership and protection of cultural heritage at the same time as museums revised their codes of practice. This in turn led to key commercially directed auction houses and dealers' associations reviewing their own codes of practice.

Deaccessioning is one of the many ethical issues facing museums in the West and one that affects the art market. It has been much in the news in recent years. In Europe the process is still comparatively rare since most museums are public institutions and their collections are guaranteed by a statute or charter. While this practice may be legally permissible in many cases it continues to attract ethical censure. In the US the situation is somewhat different and deaccessioning is more common. Since the turn of the millennium an accelerating number of private and public institutions have published codes of practice or indicated their compliance with issues pertaining to Corporate Social Responsibility (CSR). One aspect of CSR that affects public art institutions and the corporate sector is sponsorship. Major companies such as British Petroleum (BP) and Hongkong and Shanghai Banking Corporation (HSBC) sponsor both education and learning/access projects as well as exhibitions. Exhibition sponsorship is the most public-facing of these activities and can lead to both positive and negative reactions and publicity. In the UK, BP's continuing active sponsorship of exhibitions at major museums such as the British Museum and the National Portrait Gallery has attracted some criticism.

Such sponsorship is frequently an important aspect of international business and cultural diplomacy, with some companies opting to support exhibitions of art from emerging countries, thereby not only strengthening ties between cultures but also enhancing their expansion in developing countries. A case in point is HSBC's sponsorship and focus on Brazil, India and China (from 2008 to 2010) via its support of an exhibition of the work of a Brazilian artist, Ernesto Neto (b.1964), at the Hayward, its sole sponsorship of the British Museum's *Garden and Cosmos: The Royal Paintings of Jodhpur* and the Victoria and Albert Museum's *China Design Now*. The benefits go beyond that of the multinational company simply putting up the cash. Such temporary exhibitions serve mutual interests: they promote the culture of the home country and they illuminate the corporation's interest in the life and culture of the host country, thereby appealing to both constituencies. Finally this support may also function as a 'bargaining chip' and thereby benefit both sides.[4] In March 2016, BP announced that it would end its sponsorship of Tate after 26 years. This may be as a consequence of the protest by climate activists against BP as some commentators such as art collective Liberate Tate have claimed.[5]

Another key issue when considering ethical decision-making is due diligence. This is an essential part of the process of sale. It informs the activity of sellers and their intermediaries via the dealer, auction house and most importantly the buyer, in order to support and underpin the initial evaluation of the work. As Yasmin Railton demonstrates in her analysis of the conservation process, due diligence begins with a technical examination and a condition report. This may result in consultations with expert conservators, undoing the damage of previous conservation or restoration and in the case of an Old Master painting, removing significant overpainting and ensuring that all subsequent interventions are reversible. Restoration, particularly if it is non-reversible, may have a bearing on the market value of an art object. Due diligence also necessitates assessing the extent of any proposed intervention. Due diligence may shift according to the nature of the work: its age, value and location and circumstances being key determinants. Best practice also entails a careful examination of provenance, with particular steps taken to ensure that the art has not been looted, for example art that may have been subject to Nazi misappropriation, or the more recent widespread looting and destruction by Daesh. Here the motivation may be to destroy the cultural identity of statehood or to sell artefacts on the international market. Such criminal activity is analysed by Gareth Fletcher, with fascinating examples of theft by dispossession, theft by destruction and theft by deception. More recently (February 2016), the Art Loss Register located two paintings stolen from a private residence in Amsterdam in 2010. They first located the works in the catalogue of a Swiss auction house in 2014 and verified this with reference to the Interpol database. The ensuing international police investigation obliged the auction house to withdraw the works from sale.[6] An independent review in 2016 found that the National Gallery of Australia (NGA) may have been among prestigious art galleries duped by false documentation. This relates to a long-running smuggling scandal that involved temple looters in India together with a well-known New York art dealer. The NGA reported in February 2016 that it had identified 22 objects of suspect provenance in its Asian art collection including 14 works purchased from New York-based dealer Subhash Kapoor for $11 million.[7]

An attribution will frequently be found to be insecure because of a lack of consensus among experts. So due diligence is vital where larger sums are at stake, but also in the event of a law suit regarding the authenticity of the art object. Issues of due diligence intersect with authenticity and connoisseurship. With respect to art-related litigation once again we are reminded that art is different. Experts may only give evidence based on fact and this may present more challenges with respect to art where connoisseurship and the judgement of the expert are called into account. The prime issue with professional negligence cases is to decide not whether the defendant is right or wrong per se but to conclude whether the opinion given was reasonable, including whether the expert should have spent more time on due diligence to underpin that opinion. The judge is influenced by the view that s/he forms of the credibility of the experts. The issues raised by experts may prove difficult to manage. From the litigator's perspective, many major companies have 'expert witness' departments from where professionals in areas such as economic modelling or accounting may be called to give evidence. As one might expect, here again the art world is different. Judgements are more subjective – particularly with respect to connoisseurship – and there may be very few leading experts in the field. For litigators trained to present experts in an adversarial setting in order to definitely demonstrate that a painting is by the artist claimed, there is an additional problem in the working practice of art historians. In the visual arts experts in the field may consult each other and work collaboratively to reach a judgement, rather than operating independently and coming to clear black-and-white conclusions. The latter is a modus operandi that lends itself more readily than the visual arts to an adversarial courtroom process. More recently, it has been suggested that the Australian method of 'hot tubbing', in which all of the experts stand before the judge and give evidence prior to the main hearing, may indeed both constitute best practice and speed up the judicial process. Art expertise is increasingly reliant on technical assessment. It requires professionals with skills in analysing data as well as with competence in connoisseurship and the ability to assess contextual information.

Due diligence, then, may also intersect with codes of ethics as well as uncovering criminal activity involving art. The 1970 UNESCO Convention on Prohibiting and Preventing the Illicit Import, Export and Transfer of Cultural Property not only established legal requirements, but also led to ethical ones for pre-acquisition due diligence in order to ensure that artefacts illicitly traded prior to 1970 did not appear in museum collections. According to Tom Christopherson (see 'Due Diligence'), this heralded a fundamental change in both museum and market practice. Once again, we return to the question of art's distinctiveness when considering rights of artists where, as Christopherson explains, one of the key questions concerns whether artists' rights should be different from those of other professionals. Until the late twentieth century, largely in response to the Berne Convention, much of Europe and the US failed to recognise artists' moral rights. France has always held very strong views on the rights of artists. Recently there was much publicity and a storm of protest in the UK when a British collector submitted a nude that he believed to be painted by Marc Chagall to the BBC programme *Fake or Fortune*. Purchased in 1992 for £100,000, there had been doubts about the work's authenticity. It was sent to the Chagall Committee in Paris for their opinion, but the Committee ordered the work to be destroyed as a forgery.[8] Under French law this is permissible. The UK and France have different views of 'art and its creation as a form of asset, or as an entirely separate phenomenon'.

The issue of artists' copyright, appropriation, caricature or parody in future may also end up in the law courts. In the West this is usually regarded as acceptable under general principles of free speech and comment but in other parts of the world artists' rights are restricted to a greater degree. In the EU, the law concerning artists' resale rights came into force from January 2001. To date, the US has not followed, and, as with freedom of expression, copyright or moral rights, laws on this subject remain widely divergent depending on the location of the sale in spite of considerable efforts to harmonise such rights around the world.

Alongside the moral, legal and ethical issues around the making and dissemination of art and the status of artists is the relationship between the dealer and the artist, and between the dealer and collector (see Derrick Chong). Typically this relationship goes far beyond the transactional. A good dealer is committed to supporting his or her artist in numerous different ways. As well as exhibiting the work, this service could entail introducing the artist to key players in the art world, including curators, critics and collectors, so that the reputation of the artist is conscientiously considered, managed and enhanced. This may explain why a primary dealer could take a 50 per cent stake in the work and why in the age of digital platforms most artists continue to work with and through dealers. With a big name artist this service will also include management of the brand. As Chong points out, this relationship might be described as a joint venture or protracted partnership. Artists who are stars in their field may move between dealer agents and similarly rising stars may be lured away from their dealers by one of the larger international conglomerates. A respected dealer also legitimises the acquisition of a work of art. In recent years the collector–dealer relationship has been complicated by an acceleration in the scale of collecting – particularly in the contemporary art arena. Chong notes that new intermediaries can disrupt the collector–dealer relationship with collectors working with art consultants, art advisers and interior decorators. This results in the involvement of several intermediaries (all of whom will need their fee or commission) between the discovery and sale of the work of art and the collector's acquisition. Here the occasional lack of transparency may end in a law suit: Was the purchaser who thought that s/he was buying an Old Master drawing for £7 million from dealer A via a disclosed intermediary adviser B aware that there were other advisers assisting with locating an appropriate example, advisors C, D and E and scouring the planet for the desired object, each of whom received a fee?

More recently auction houses have challenged the position of dealers and eroded the boundaries between what were formerly distinct and different modi operandi by behaving more like dealers. This includes private treaty sales by auction houses which thereby mimic dealers' transactions, or auction houses buying dealerships or opening commercial galleries. Cases in point include Christie's' purchase of Haunch of Venison in London (2007–13) and Sotheby's opening of a contemporary space, S2 in New York (2011) and London (2013), in order to enhance their reach to the market and appeal further to collectors. Some dealers appear to mimic practices associated more often with public museums and galleries – they include works on display that are not for sale and present themed exhibitions that may come from both private and public collections and include a scholarly catalogue. In addition, dealers may insist that works for sale are of 'museum quality', indicating that they are premier works of art. Such practices enhance their reputation and brand and are designed to appeal further to their collectors. Both collectors and buyers of art frequently prefer the auction process to other forms of procurement since there is a perception that this is more transparent. David Bellingham unpacks the complex nature of the auction process. In theory an art auction is open to all but, as Bellingham argues, this is not always the case since the auction remains a complex process of social interaction requiring specialist knowledge and risk management. To the uninitiated, the art auction is a minefield in which the reserve price remains undisclosed but will never be higher than the low estimate cited in the catalogue. To those in the know the auctioneer will signal that the reserve price has been reached by noting aloud 'I can sell . . .' To further complicate matters, the auctioneer will have a confidential log book in which absentee or commission bids are recorded and it is the auctioneer's responsibility to bid on behalf of absentees. As well as phone bids there is live online internet bidding.

This book sets out to cast light on many of the significant areas that apply to art business and the professional art world across both the public and private domain. We focus on the many interactions that take place in the making, evaluating, collecting, buying and selling of the art object and together we hope that they will provide an insight into the inconstant world of art business.

Jos Hackforth-Jones and Iain Robertson

1   Ellis, Adrian, 'The problem with privately funded museums', *The Art Newspaper*, issue 188, February 2008, p.24

2   The reader should be made aware of what we mean by category, sector (sub-sectors or types) and commodity. A category refers to a basket of related goods, for example paintings, drawings and sculpture. A sector refers to a department of that category, for example Old Master paintings. A type or sub-sector might be the Italian School of painting or the paintings of Raphael. A commodity is a single painting. In the relatively new, materially various and evolutionary sector of contemporary art, art that appears in international and national art fairs, which is referred to in Iain Robertson's essay on 'Art Fairs' and which is held by alpha-delta art dealers and auctioned by tier one and two auction houses, forms the sector contemporary art. A sub-sector in this market might be photography and contemporary design.

3   Singer, L.P., and G. Lynch, 'Public Choice in the Tertiary Art Market', *Journal of Cultural Economics*, 1994, vol.18, no.3

4   See Natasha Degen, 'National Authenticity on Display? Exhibiting Art from Emerging Markets' in Megan Aldrich and Jos Hackforth-Jones, *Art and Authenticity*, LH and SIA, 2012

5   *Guardian*, 11 March 2016

6 'Stolen Dutch Paintings Found in a Swiss Auction', *Antiques Trade Gazette*, 22 February 2016

7 *Nikkei Asian Review,* 26 February 2016

8 *Apollo,* 4 March 2014

Note on currencies

We have adjusted historic prices to current values, taking into account inflation and the cost of living, throughout the text from 1760 to the present day. We have converted all national currencies to US dollars after October 1986, the date of the sudden deregulation of the London stock market. With the exception of Japanese Yen between 1987 and 1990, the primary currency in the international market from the 1980s until today has been the US dollar. Before the 1980s we have not converted an adjusted value in a national currency to an adjusted value in US dollars. With distant historic values (eighteenth- and nineteenth-century) we have converted national currencies (including US dollars) into pounds sterling because the international market operated out of London. For seventeenth-century prices we have converted transactions into Dutch guilders or florins but would not attempt to construct an adjusted price. This reflects the central position of the United Provinces in the art trade during this period.

THE BIGGER PICTURE

GLOBALISATION OF
THE ART MARKET

It is a common belief amongst nations that rely on international trade that mutual economic embeddedness is a virtue. These nations are at the helm of all of our global institutions. However, economic integration is not so much a virtue as a necessity for these states and so the common-good aspect of the term is often overstated. Economic over-reliance on other territories will result in universally shared 'panics', which have visited the late modern world four times in the twentieth century (1903, 1907, 1919 and 1973), although a crash and a structural economic and political shift, such as in 1929, is more rare. The global art commodity market was initiated by the European nation states that established the first joint-stock companies with overseas 'interests'; the Dutch United East India Company (1602) and the English Honourable East India Company (1600) being the two largest and furthest-reaching. This liminal state required the concatenation of military and political attributes before cultural superiority could be added as the final act of global hegemony. The opportunity to change the world order in favour of the maritime trading nations of the Netherlands and Britain was encouraged by a particular notion of freedom.

In his book *An Essay Concerning Human Understanding* (1689), the philosopher John Locke (1632–1704) strenuously examines the concept of individual choice or volition. Thus, a free man who chooses luxury and debauchery over study and knowledge is no less happier than his counter-part who does the reverse. The fierce, empirical logic of Locke allows for a great degree of moral relativism. The amount of freedom which Locke allows us, has, it can be argued, moved mankind from an antinomian mind-set to a casuistical one. The uneasiness of mind in want of an absent good that Locke attributes to our will and which prompts our desire, he explains, gives rise to the spring of action. At its outer limits, a desire for honour, power or riches, he calls a fantastical uneasiness. When a man is content, he asks rhetorically, what action or will is there left? Locke's philosophy certainly complements the energy with which the Dutch and the English set about being individually industrious and independent; be it in carrying goods across the oceans from a producer to a consumer or manufacturing basic and luxury goods. The ships built in England and the Netherlands scuppered the global ambitions of the greatest contemporary power, Spain. Locke argued that the moral relativism or individual freedom to decide what good is desired can be interpreted by each person according to their moral compass, or short-term blindness as to the eventual good. It can be suggested that the unofficially sanctioned depredations that were visited on the Spanish plate fleet and galleons by English men-of-war and Dutch 'sea-beggars' respectively were acts in the interest of a future greater (national) good. The officially sanctioned trading conglomerates in the north of India, Java and Bali which ultimately formed the backbone of imperial empires for both nations were more permanent examples of the results of the same uneasiness and thirst for individual good and collective improvement.

Locke, widely regarded as the 'father of the enlightenment', lived in both England and the Netherlands, in which country he mixed with the many radical Protestant groups that had provided intellectual succour to the philosopher Baruch Spinoza (1632–77). In Locke's book, his chapter 'Of Power' really provides an intellectual pretext for the political authority that both nations would enjoy for the next hundred or more years. A quasi-scientific explanation of the causality of movement mimicked the methods by which the British crown first unseated the Mughals and then successively displaced the sub-continent's many rulers. Today we would call it the political momentum encapsulated in domino theory. Locke's expression of freedom as individual consciousness, realised as the desire of a man to move or not to move, culminated in the idea that it is impossible to be more free than to have the power to do what you will. This emphasis on self-determination had an impact on the methods by which both nations embarked on their future period of territorial aggrandisement. Locke likens the desire – which is an uneasiness of mind – for want of an absent good to a pain stimulating action towards short-term satisfaction or, more sensibly, long-term good.

The individual moral philosophy of Locke, which found expression in the perceived fairness or at least justification of the administration of the British Empire, might be usefully contrasted with the antinomian and patently unfair approach adopted by the Spanish conquistadors in the Indies. In 1513, a jurist, Juan López de Palacios Rubios (1450–1524), drew up a document known as the 'Requirement', which began with a history of time from Adam to a grant made by the Pope to the Castilian crown. It obliged every Indian to obey the crown on pain of horrible death. The Spanish diarist Bartolomé de las Casas (1484–1566) declares this to be one of the crassest instances of legalism in European history. It is indeed a perfect example of a *fait accompli*, without even a vestige of intellectual justification. The account of Spanish atrocities in the Indies by Las Casas was used by Anglo-Dutch propagandists to blacken the reputation of Spanish imperialism from the sixteenth to eighteenth centuries, until the age of the Protestant empires.

Eighteenth-century political change in Europe aided the cause of the discontented bourgeoisie. The prolonged financial collapse of the monarchy in France, which began with the Mississippi Bubble (1718–20), culminated in King Louis XVI convoking the Estates General (1787) and demanding the payment to the crown of millions of livres. The subsequent French Revolution (1789) opened the doors to political emancipation. In England, the Acts of Union with Scotland (1706/7), victory over the Mughals at the Battle of Plassey (1757), the sales of the art collections of the Duc d'Orléans (1792–1802) and victory over France and her allies at the Battle of Waterloo (1815) marked Britain's concomitant rise to global authority.

Cultural globalisation, evident in homogenised commodities labelled by styles of art, has grown out of the economic union of states and their conglomerates. The international art market is the instrument through which global culture finds its ultimate expression. A painting, for better or for worse, has become the ultimate global possession and it is priced accordingly; for example *Les Femmes D'Alger (Version O)* (1955) by Pablo Picasso (1881–1973) achieved a price of $179.3 million at Christie's, New York in May 2015. But are we now in the state of economic sepulchre before revivification, or is the world about to change? Is globalisation a thing of the past or, more likely, is it about to change face?

The dissolution of the Ottoman Empire after the First World War saw the last significant vestige of 'Oriental' power edited from globalisation. The Orientalist painting style is the visual embowering of the East. The appropriation of African (and other) cultural tropes by late modernist European artists is, by its very act, misappropriation and humiliation. The slow dissolution of the Orient had begun in the art world with the schooling in their respective homelands by European masters of the Indian artist Raja Ravi Varma (1848–1906), the Philippine artist Fernando Amorsolo (1892–1972) and the Indonesian Raden Saleh (1811–80) in the European Academic oil painting tradition. More fortunate artists from outside Europe would be instructed, like the Chinese oil painter Xu Beihong (1895–1953), in Paris at the Ecole Nationale Supérieure des Beaux-Arts, and others like the inventive Pan Yuliang (1895–1977) would become sufficiently esteemed to teach at the Ecole des Beaux-Arts. Pan is credited with her Shanghai contemporary Liu Haisu (1896–1994), with introducing French impressionism to China. Of course there were nationalist artistic movements even in the early years of this European cultural *imperium*, such as the early twentieth-century *Lingnan* School in China and the late-nineteenth century *nihon-ga* School in Japan, but they failed to stem the universal accedence to Western modernism.

An art made in the language of the global art world today, to be consumed by those weaned on arbitrary Western 'standards' with its local cultural characteristics, signals a certain acknowledgement of two things: that other cultures are integral to globalisation, and more importantly, that by this act of concession, a transition of power is taking place in its broadest sense. This rearguard action by the Western art world seeks to protect a vestige of the great cultural capital it has accumulated over the last few centuries. Of course another reading might be that amidst the clangour of the assimilation of the Communist world into the global fold in 1989, the presiding consensus has accommodated so much polarity that its actual form has been lost. We will see how this condition, perhaps induced by decadence, can equally be applied to art and creativity today.

What are the changes to the art world that will take place in the wake of this transition? The beginnings of this passing may have been felt during the second significant economic tremor of the twentieth century in 1987.

Shortly thereafter, Japanese corporations, that were the largest single art market buyers, left the market after paying exorbitant sums of money in a febrile market for unimpressive impressionist and post-impressionist pictures by familiar European artists. The Japanese buyers have not returned since to the international art market in these numbers. The Japanese market has, with the exception of the Shinwa auction house (Tokyo) and one or two internationally conformist contemporary artists, sought refuge in its own arrangement: a rigid system of art exchange around the Tokyo Art Club known as *kokankai*, in which prices are pre-determined by a cartel of dealers. This system and the nation's indigenous art forms of craft and *nihon-ga* (painting technique) militate against the international art market and by extension globalisation.

China and other lesser emerging art markets have been encouraged to contribute their own brand of contemporary art and their necessary instruments to the global convocation in the form of artists, art, galleries, museums, art fairs and collectors. However most Chinese interest has been sparked by indigenous modern and Old Master paintings and bibelots made from jade, stone, ceramic and wood. In Russia, India and Indonesia the irresolute acceptance of indigenous international contemporary art suggests that these cultures will refute the West's global cultural assertions. India's art market has been forced to trade in the Modernist aesthetic bequeathed by Jawaharlal Nehru (1889–1964) because of national laws prohibiting the commercial exchange in antiquities and religious artefacts. Its art world has remained untouched by globalisation. There are very few *kunsthallen* on the sub-continent and even dealers and art fairs selling the latest cutting-edge contemporary art are conspicuously absent. Iran, in spite of its efforts to solicit the immediate approbation of the West through the use of its hoard of post-war Western painting and sculpture acquired by the displaced ruling Pahlavi family (1925–79), in common with other significant regional cultures, is now beginning a rapid detachment from Western aesthetics and standards. In fact, Iran would be well advised to sell its art stockpile while the unit values are high.

If one form of globalisation is dying, what will replace it? China and other emerging markets have experienced economic travails since 2011. The West's art world has lauded those artists from different cultures who have subscribed to a neoliberal cultural consensus. The Chinese artists Zhu Wou-ki (1921–2013) and Zhu Dequn (1920–2014) are lionised for their Klee-like abstractions; the Political Pop oil painters from Beijing and Chongqing have received huge sums of money for their work, while the art works of the Iranians Farhad Moshiri (b.1963) and Shirin Neshat (b.1957) have, together with those of the super-realist Turkish painter Taner Ceylan (b.1967), received plaudits from the international art world and high prices on its market.

In short, the art world has accommodated as much material and even ideology as it can, while at the same time maintaining equilibrium. It is extraordinary how dramatically different the intention, appearance and exhibition of works of art are today in internationally inspired galleries, festivals and arenas. It is, therefore, equally astounding how the art world is able to claim all this material as its own. This art may be found at the Venice Biennale, Documenta and in *kunsthallen* in Europe and in America. This high-end commodity is often site-specific, engaged with its context and sometimes very large. It purports to contain a meaning far beyond the constraints of its material or historical significance. A good example (and there are many) was an exhibition curated by Norman Rosenthal (b.1944) on materiality in the work of Joseph Beuys (1921–86) in the Parisian Marais district branch of Galerie Thaddaeus Ropac in 2012. The space given to Beuys revisited the artist's performance in which he walked across a stage with a horse, banging a cymbal and reciting parts of Shakespeare's play *Titus Andronicus*. The cymbals were part of *Missa Solemnis* at his final exhibition at the Palazzo Reale in Naples in 1985 where they were placed in a vitrine with the artist's fur coat and a cast of a head. For the Paris show, a white horse and all the other material elements of this performance were collected for display. The art market has been slower to react than the art world; the value of Beuys's art is low. Few emerging market galleries and inconsiderable amounts of work by artists from outside the West have been exhibited at global art fairs. The art worlds of Moscow, Beijing, New Delhi, Tehran and Mexico City have given little support to their respective international art market havens or to the promotion of the global Western aesthetic (with local characteristics) outside of their territories.

There are several vantage points from which to spy the future. Each gives a different view of the unfolding scene. The East's view is that an entente cordiale between Russia, China, Pakistan and Iran heralds a new world order. The statistics of this supposed entente overwhelmingly favour this orientation: China alone comprises 1.34 billion people, a combined GDP of $12.7 trillion and a land mass of 29.13 million square kilometres. Two policy initiatives, in particular, overseen by the incumbent Chinese leader, Xi Jinping (b.1953), appear to support the outward expression of this alliance of states: the abolition of the one-child and *yidai yilu* (one belt, one road) policies aimed at connectivity. Predictably, both are aimed at the export of labour and capital, which will inevitably lead to political influence and cultural resurgence. There is an equally robust counter-narrative. In 2007 President Hu Jintao had declared that the great rejuvenation of the Chinese nation would be accompanied by cultural power, which affords both cultural cohesion and strength. China, Iran and Pakistan have the deepest and most enduring relationship with Central Asia and with good reason argue that this arrangement reflects the legitimate balance of power. History, size of population and economic ascendancy are introduced to justify their claims. The West's view is that the new policy and alliance is built on disaffection and internal frailty. The Chinese economy is growing at a slower rate than at any time since the economic reforms of 1979. Russia and Pakistan have weak economies and Iran is divided between a powerful conservative constituency that seeks to reassert traditionalism and a young generation that the government deems to have been seduced by Western consumerism. The country is anxious to rid itself of the Western economic embargo, but fearful of the negative social effects of too much liberalism.

It can be argued that China's current policy is constructed out of a fear of *neiluan* (internal disorder) and *waihuan* (external threat). The key 'soft' weapon in the West's armoury is that of individual liberty. China, Russia, Pakistan and Iran 'behave' in a contrary way towards their citizens to the global 'norm'; three of the governments in the new alliance are democratic, but not democratic enough. This, the West concludes, compromises and even illegitimises the claims of any one of these states to a universal culture. The great population of the emerging economic world, especially in East Asia, is an actual disadvantage and de-stimulant because it prevents per capita rates from rising significantly. The key lesson learnt from the Industrial Revolution and which is apparent in today's world of technology is that population does not necessarily equate with real wealth and power. The United States accounts for 5 per cent of the world's population and 21 per cent of its GDP. In contrast, East Asia (excluding Japan) contains 60 per cent of the world's people and generates 30 per cent of its output.

A salient statistic in favour of a new globalisation, nevertheless, is fiscal wealth. China and Japan held $4.45 trillion in foreign exchange reserves at the end of 2015. This figure rises to nearly $6 trillion when other regional states (and Singapore) are added. In contrast, only Switzerland amongst European states holds more than $200 billion in foreign reserves. The world's emerging economies also have vast sovereign wealth funds. Numbers of high net worth individuals in East Asia and the Middle East have both grown dramatically faster than those in Europe (East Asia 9.7 per cent in 2010 and 8.5 per cent in 2014, Middle East 10.4 per cent in 2010 and 7.7 per cent in 2014). It is the global spending power of 4.69 million wealthy East Asians in particular that determines cultural spending – and therefore cultural direction – in great measure and the nature of globalisation. A caveat to this argument is that the political alignment of East Asia fails to reflect its cultural similarity, and this, together with India's opprobrium towards China and open hostility towards Pakistan, grants the presiding global status quo more time.

If there is a work of art that marks the changing economic fortunes in a late modern world, it is *The Finding of Moses* (1904) by Lawrence Alma-Tadema (1836–1912). The painting was commissioned by the English civil engineer Sir John Aird, who paid the artist £5,250, the equivalent of £390,000 today. The work declined in value following the death of Alma-Tadema, until the 1960s, when it was acquired for a mere £252 (equivalent today to £7,775). And yet, following the revival of Alma-Tadema's reputation at the 1973 exhibition *Victorians in Togas* at the Metropolitan Museum of Art, it was bought in 1995 by a private collector in the US for $2.5 million. In 2010 it sold in New York to a Chinese collector for nearly $36 million.

The proposition that there is a need to square politics, economics and the military with culture is often occluded. There is a view that globalisation is an ideology of free, inevitable progression towards human betterment, and hand in hand with that belief, that commodities and leisure are pursuits that incrementally resolve our needs. The economic law of marginal diminishing returns suggests that there is a point at which consumption has a deleterious effect upon us. Culture, characterised by the 'high arts', appears to offer a solution, in the sense that it rewards the spirit more than the body. In all this we should not lose sight of the fact that the art traded on the global art market is a commodity, and as such is a reflection of the current form of globalisation.

Iain Robertson

Bibliography

Barclays World Insights, *Profit or Pleasure? Exploring the Motivations behind Treasure Trends*, Barclays Capital, 2012

Bongard, Willy, 'Kunst Kompass', Capital, published annually

Citigroup, 'Plutonomy: Buying Luxury, Explaining Global Imbalances', Citigroup, 16 October 2005

Crump, Thomas, *Asia-Pacific: A History of Empire and Conflict*, Hambledon Continuum, 2007

Chu, Yin-wah and Siu-lun Wong (eds), *East Asia's New Democracies: Deepening, Reversal, Non-Liberal Alternatives*, Routledge, 2010

De Bary, Theodore (ed.), *Sources of East Asian Tradition*, Columbia University Press, 2008

Doniger, Wendy, *The Hindus: An Alternative History*, Viking/Penguin 2009

Ferguson, Niall, *The Cash Nexus: Money and Power in the Modern World 1700–2000*, Allen Lane/Penguin Books, 2001

Fukuyama, Francis, *The End of History and the Last Man*, Penguin, 1992

Hobbes, Thomas, *Leviathan*, Penguin Classics, 1985

Locke, John, *An Essay Concerning Human Understanding*, Penguin Books, 1997, see in particular the chapter 'Of Power'

ETHICS

Ethical issues have acquired an increasingly high profile in the art world over the last generation, generating a higher level of debate both among participants within the art world itself and among a widening range of commentators on that world. This has been driven, in part, by eye-catching high prices at the top end of the art market, which in themselves create reportage and discussion, and partly by changing attitudes to national patrimony and culture in museums and beyond. Broadly speaking, debate continues between those adhering to the general concept of 'the world museum' and those favouring the retention of objects in, or their return to, their place of origin. This development of discussion and review in recent years has opened up fundamental questions about the roles of law and ethics in the art world (the term 'the art world' for the purposes of this discussion encompasses both the art market and the wider network of museum and curatorial relationships and practices).

In spite of the media attention devoted to high-selling trophy objects, the annual turnover of art, both national and international, has long been financially insignificant relative to the world of international commerce and high finance. Historically, with fiscal and governmental attention more profitably directed to areas such as stock and bond markets where the financial stakes were much higher, relatively few laws were created specifically targeting the art world. In many areas (particularly in the US and UK) the art world was therefore left effectively to decide for itself how such laws, and more general laws of commerce and ownership, should be applied in practice to the attribution, ownership and movement of art. This lack of governmental scrutiny in many parts of the world, and the fragmentary nature of international law in this field, may have encouraged some art world participants in the past to adopt what some might judge a laissez-faire attitude to such matters, or at least in certain quarters to take the view that the art world was different and free to adopt its own rules and understandings. The development of the art world in this manner was assisted by the opacity of many of its transactions and relationships. Furthermore, many of these opaque transactions were carried out between small and closely-knit groups, with the emergence of common practices and rules that were locally understood and accepted by the participants, although largely unknown outside the group or trading environment concerned. The art world was therefore populated by a series of geographical or societal groups, in which insiders operated at an advantage over outsiders, with knowledge in an opaque world representing an important premium. The general lack of transparency, combined with the absence of a specific legal framework for art business, arguably enhanced the feeling, or perhaps the subconscious assumption, that parts of the art world were governed by laws and ethical codes that were different from conventional commercial transactions and relationships, thus allowing participants to set their own boundaries or at the extreme to operate in what outsiders might consider to be a virtual ethical vacuum.

Several factors have emerged over the last fifty years or so to challenge the historical position. On the one hand, transnational responses to the sourcing, acquisition and movement of items of cultural heritage have developed in both legal and ethical spheres. This can be traced back to the 1954 Convention for the Protection of Cultural Property in the Event of Armed Conflict and its subsequent protocols (The Hague Convention), but it gained real impetus following the 1970 UNESCO Convention on the Means of Prohibiting and Preventing the Illicit Import, Export and Transfer of Ownership of Cultural Property, and the 1972 Convention Concerning the Protection of the World Cultural and Natural Heritage. These conventions and their successors were not immediately or universally adopted, and even when adopted, included reservations and restrictions which led some to question the extent of their practical and legal effect. However their creation and steady implementation did lead to the development of a wider application of common ethical standards; an illustration of this would be the museums' codes of practice on due diligence, purchasing and display of their collections, largely developed since the 1970s. These codes of practice in turn influenced the policies and codes of conduct of higher-profile participants in the art market such as the major auction houses and dealer associations.

Another instrument of change affecting the historical structures of the art world, and influencing its response to ethical issues, has been the development of global communications, transactions and relationships, particularly over the last twenty years. The process of globalisation of the art world, especially at the higher-value end of the art market, has threatened the historically cosy world of the local insider. Domestic markets can no longer rely on mutual understanding and interest but are subject to more formal regulation and practice, and local and national structures have been under pressure to embrace and cater for an increasing range of outsiders in order to compete for the benefits of a larger and wider market. This process is by no means universal or complete, but in the larger international markets it has underpinned a movement, in legal and wider ethical terms, towards a more clearly defined set of rules to govern duties and expectations in a multinational marketplace. This, alongside the growth of information available on the internet, has in turn generated a greater degree of transparency. Although elements of the art world continue to be more opaque than some other commercial sectors, these factors have contributed to the development of a wider awareness and discussion of the ethics underpinning art world transactions.

Business ethics have always involved a dialogue between the moral rights of various stakeholders. The economist Milton Friedman (1912–2006) took the absolutist ethical stance of pragmatism, arguing that it is the duty of a business to maximise the financial profits of its stakeholders, so long as it remains within the law. Friedman argued that it was the duty of governments to create suitable laws, thereby implicitly condoning potentially immoral, but legal, business activity. Historically many, if not most, participants in the art world appeared to favour this approach, and many still do. In recent years, however, with the increase in ethical global awareness and a wider general discussion about issues such as participation, interest and involvement, the definition of 'interested stakeholders' has broadened for all activities to include any person, plant, animal or other natural object directly or indirectly affected by the business or proposal. When a new airport for London was proposed for the Thames estuary, for instance, the ethical debate about the human, floral and faunal stakeholders was given as much weight in the media as the arguments about financial cost and benefit. The threats to marshland wildlife habitats and villages played an important role in the wider discussion. Similarly in the art world, today's ethical debates embrace financial stakeholders and also other interested parties, both human, animal and natural, with a recognised need to consider a significantly wider range of national, ethnological, cultural and historical interests than would have been the case for previous generations. Laws, in general, continue to follow national boundaries, even when nations have come together to agree common principles in international conventions and treaties. The debate about ethical values however is less constrained, either by approach or geography, sometimes leaving national laws to catch up.

Ethical issues and dilemmas in the art world are now everyday news, from widespread destruction or looting of cultural heritage through terrorism and warfare and the emergence of unprovenanced works of antiquity divorced from their historical context, to the destruction of elephants for their ivory for 'medicinal purposes'. This last case serves as an example of the tension between the ethical positions taken by absolutists and relativists. The absolutist argues for a complete ban on all trade and movement of ivory of any period or age, whether carved or not. The relativist argues for a cut-off date to preserve the trade in old ivory (which for centuries found its way into many items of furniture, jewellery and decorative art). Both positions are based upon recognition of the need to preserve important endangered species such as the elephant or rhinoceros from extinction by a seemingly insatiable poaching industry. Coming into force in 1975, the Convention on the International Trade in Endangered Species of Wild Fauna and Flora (CITES) introduced a licensing and control regime covering the movement and sale of more than 35,000 species of flora and fauna, with a ban on the trade in materials such as ivory unless there is proof that the item in question had been 'worked' (carved or moulded so as to be significantly altered from its natural state) before 1947, such as an ivory snooker ball produced in 1900. The debate about the ethics and practicalities of countering the poaching threat is ongoing, and the interpretation and application of the CITES regime has undergone constant change over recent years to keep up. Exports of rhinoceros horn within the EU, for example, have recently been declared illegal with very limited exceptions (and regardless of whether the horn is old or modern, worked or unworked) even though it remains legal to own and sell worked rhinoceros horn within the UK, with an appropriate permit. There is currently a fierce debate about the ethics and consequences of a complete ban in all trade of ivory and horn, from the proposition of a legalised and controlled ivory trade to combat more effectively the threat of the illegal trade, to the ethics of undermining rights of ownership and trade by banning the sale of antique ivory for which no contemporary elephant has been killed, and arguably for which no contemporary elephant would be saved. The ethical debate is matched by calls in the US and EU to introduce a legal prohibition on all sales of ivory, regardless of age, provenance or form, but as with other ethical questions at play in the art world, there is much to be said on both sides.

The Elgin Marbles debate offers an example of the various conflicting ethical issues involved in the aftermath of the removal of cultural property from its original location. Some argue that the British saved the sculptures from inevitable destruction, and therefore have an ethical right to keep them. They also argue that they retain legal title because an official document was provided giving Thomas Bruce, 7th Earl of Elgin, the right to remove the marbles, which he did from 1801 to 1812. Others argue that this document was agreed with the Turks, who were an occupying force in Greece, and that subsequent Greek liberation annuls any Turkish legal agreements. Ethically, they argue that the marbles should now be returned to Greece as a more fitting home for these site-specific sculptures. As for archaeological objects that have been illegally excavated and thus lack provenance, dealers argue that it is ethically preferable to continue to trade them because their financial value at least means that they are cared for. Archaeologists, however, argue that this trade condones and encourages further illegal excavations and exports of objects of high cultural value. In the past, in order to cope with these types of issue, many art businesses traditionally adopted Friedman's pragmatist ethics, and unlike higher-profile financial business sectors, their actions drew little serious response from governments. However, with the development of the internet and 'globalised comment' this approach is becoming more difficult to sustain, and within the narrow confines of the art world itself, behaviour deemed to be unethical is increasingly recognised as likely to have significant and adverse consequences. A major component in this development within the art world has been the power of 'brand' and the threat of reputational damage. After all, art is seen as one of the primary signifiers of a civilised society and dealings relating to art, whether in a market or curatorial setting, are increasingly seen as requiring a standard of ethical behaviour. Brands have a widespread recognition in art and art world participants are acutely conscious of these heightened expectations.

How do art businesses address the threat of potentially unethical behaviour? Since its origins in the ancient Greek world, the philosophical branch of ethics has addressed both individual and collective human morality in relation to civic duties and social interactions. In its definition of ethics, the *Oxford English Dictionary* refers to rules of conduct instituted by associations or other bodies. It is these rules of conduct that have often been adopted by art businesses, either individually or through membership of professional and trade associations, as a necessary but positive response to the absence or limited scope of directly relevant and applicable laws governing the art world. Codes of conduct may be comprised of strict regulations of professional practice, violations of which may lead to dismissal from the association, or in the case of an individual company, dismissal of an employee from their employment. Codes of conduct may also encompass wider, more aspirational elements, seeking to reach a higher ethical level of conduct, but (recognising that different circumstances may require a different response) falling short of a precise definition of requirements or consequence. Thus codes of practice and codes of conduct are quasi-legal and quasi-ethical in their intentions and solutions.

Reported violations of these professional ethical codes are relatively rare, and often quite shocking in their media revelation. In 2006, Bury Museum in England was stripped of its official museum status after Bury Metropolitan Borough Council sold an L.S. Lowry painting in order to balance the council's books. Accreditation for public museums (and therefore access to public funds) in the UK was awarded by the Museum, Libraries and Archives Council (MLA) (now Arts Council England) and the museum was deemed to have contravened the MLA's code of ethics, which states: 'The removal of an object ... from a museum collection must *only* be undertaken with a full understanding of the significance of the item, its character (renewable or non-renewable), legal standing, and *any loss of public trust that might result from such an action*' (our italics). This provides a good example of the way in which ethics and the ethical debate go beyond the confines of the law. Although the sale of the Lowry was legal and indeed a clear economic success, with the work selling for over twice its auction estimate at $1.85 million, the public reputation of Bury Museum was damaged and the museum lost its extremely important right to apply for MLA funding, as the MLA deemed that there had been a 'loss of public trust' in the museum through the failure of the council-owned museum to consult with the people of Bury. The Northampton Museum lost its accreditation in similar circumstances for the sale of a Sekhemka statue at Christie's in 2014. Similar issues have proved equally controversial in the US where, for instance, the Detroit Institute of Arts (2013) and the Rose Art Museum at Brandeis University (2009) faced significant public and professional outcry when financial imperatives prompted the legal owners of the museums to decide to sell all or a large part of their collections.

Most businesses operating in the art world are small owner-operated dealerships, conservators and the like, which means that the ethical considerations of the business are strongly influenced by the personal morality of the individual concerned. The variation in degrees of pricing transparency among dealerships, for instance, results partly from a lack of regulation requiring publication of prices and also from the personal approach of the dealer to the art of selling art. Many galleries do not display prices and therefore the experienced art dealer and collector retains an advantage over the uninitiated; to some this might be unethical, to others a natural consequence of one party's greater knowledge and understanding of the work and its market. Selection committees for the vetting of works of art for display and sale at art fairs have been another area of friction. These committees often comprise (largely, if not exclusively) the participating dealers themselves, leading to claims of potential conflict of interest and unethical practice in the selection of other dealers and their wares to be represented at the fairs. The counter-argument would be that the participation of dealers provides the most accurate assessment of the participants and their works of art, by people with current and practical experience of the objects and fairs concerned, for the protection of those attending and buying at the fair. Again, in the absence of specific regulation, the success or otherwise of the fair organiser in explaining these processes and convincing outsiders of their ethical and effective application could be a significant influence on the brand and reputation of the fair and ultimately its commercial success.

Public museums have also been accused of unethical selection processes, with purchase committees operating behind closed doors and including private collectors and even the artists themselves. When the British artist Chris Ofili (b.1968) was serving as a trustee of Tate Modern in 2006, the gallery purchased his composite work *The Upper Room* for $791,190. The Tate was criticised by the Charity Commission for a potential conflict of interest in the manner of its acquisition of the work of a serving trustee. Eventually, and after considerable public comment – perhaps in part based upon the fact that over 250,000 members of the public had viewed the work at Tate from 2005–6 – it was considered that the wider public benefit of the acquisition outweighed any concerns arising from the process leading to the acquisition. The incident nevertheless led to several museums reviewing their policies and practices for the roles of trustees and the dealings of purchase committees. Notwithstanding, the world's most important contemporary art museums often include private collectors and other interested parties on their art selection committees in order to access their privileged knowledge of the art concerned and the markets in which it can be obtained. This is particularly true for unexposed artists from emerging nations, such as those of Latin America, where such practical knowledge may be held in few hands. It creates potential for an ethical conflict of interest: on one hand the private collectors may have a vested interest in placing works by artists (in whose other works they have invested) in important public collections because of the validation of such works that this would bring. On the other hand, failure to utilise such exclusive and expert knowledge of an emerging market where such knowledge is in limited supply might render the institution liable to the charge that it has overpaid for a work or acquired a work of lesser importance. In this, as in many other instances in the art world, the key lies in a considered procedure which is as transparent as possible, so that the different attributes of each case can be objectively and consistently taken into account, and the decision adequately communicated to interested parties. It is also true that one rule or principle does not fit all cases, and it is extremely difficult to apply a simple ethical principle to a diverse range of possible circumstances.

With the increasingly complex global nature of art dealing and the very high returns sometimes available, the law around the world has started to take a more robust and concerted approach to this part of the art business than had previously been the case, particularly in issues such as money-laundering, art theft and looting works of antiquity. The list of countries ratifying the 1970 UNESCO Convention, for example, has grown beyond the original 'source nations' with a rich cultural heritage such as India, Italy, Greece and Turkey. They have been joined more recently by 'market nations' such as the UK and Switzerland (the US did sign the Convention in 1983, but with the important proviso that implementation would be down to the decisions of its individual states). While conventions such as UNESCO 1970 create obligations between states, as opposed to rights directly enforceable by individuals, the period has also seen a growing willingness by national courts to take heed of, and enforce, the laws of patrimony of other states in an increasing number of cases. Beyond the enforcement of patrimony laws in the courts, the Conventions and the environment they created have encouraged a wider ethical discussion beyond the confines of the law. A case in point was the 1998 'Washington Principles on Nazi-Confiscated Art', issued by delegates at the Washington Conference that year, and which opened the way to nearly two decades in which national records have been researched and settlements negotiated to enable the return of works looted in Europe between 1933 and 1945, despite the legal barriers of limitation periods and the like.

Issues of conservation and authenticity are also ethically interconnected. If an art object is poorly restored, its wider authenticity can be called into question because its pristine condition is more or less compromised and possibly effectively metamorphosed into a new work of art. To deal with the ethics of conservation first, there are two opposing sides in the ethical debate, relating to the commercial art market on the one hand and the academically curated museum on the other. In the latter, the current ethical codes on museum conservation as published by the International Council of Museums (ICOM) stress the importance of non-intrusive methods and materials, based upon the avoidance of any interference with the material object other than to extend its life for future generations. For instance, adhesives employed in restoration work must be non-damaging as well as totally reversible, so that the object is not damaged in any future deconstruction and restructuring. Restored areas must be totally visible, so that the conserved object is an honest composite of original authentic parts together with added modern restorative materials. The ethics of museum conservation have developed in the last generation, with a tendency towards greater transparency. While fragmentary ancient Greek vases in the British Museum were formerly glued back together with damaging and discolouring insoluble animal-based adhesives, today conservation-standard soluble epoxy resins are employed. Any gaps left in the reconstructed vase would previously have been filled in with plaster and painted to fit in with the rest of the decoration; today a monochrome plaster similar to the surrounding local colours would be employed to demonstrate clearly the restored parts of the vase. A similar vase on the art market, however, might still be restored in the more traditional approach described above, rather than conserved, in order to enhance its commercial value. In other words, the object could be intrusively (and arguably unethically) transformed from its fragmentary state into a composite of original and modern materials with no attempt to indicate the material differences to the viewer, with missing pieces painted to match the original decoration and the entire object given a pristine appearance. This practice has old roots, with sellers and buyers on the Grand Tour in eighteenth-century Italy happy to improve or copy ancient pieces for the benefit of better display. Art collectors are, however, becoming increasingly aware of museums' judgement that the nature of such restorations may be unethical, and some now tend to avoid over-restored objects. Increasingly, dealers may be seen to use a discussion of the ethics of the conservation process as part of a positive sales pitch, in the same way as they might now draw attention to the strong provenance of an antique work. On a pragmatic level, it might be said that an ethical non-intrusive conservation strategy, being based on purely curatorial principles, should mean that the art object will survive in a better state and therefore retain its financial value for a much longer period. However there is also a perceived commercial value in the ethical approach to conservation, in its own right.

Different ethical principles are associated with different types of art object. For example, whereas in the Renaissance top sculptors were also employed as restorers of broken antique statues, fulfilling the modern role of the conservator, nowadays collectors have a strong aesthetic preference for the headless and limbless torso or the portrait bust lacking a nose, clearly representing as it does the virgin condition of the piece. This approach is less common among purchasers of antique furniture.

The ethics of authenticity affect the art world in various ways. Most obviously, fakes and forgeries present a major problem to dealers, museums and collectors alike. The forged art work breaches various laws around the world if it can be shown to be a deliberate attempt to deceive the buyer into paying an enhanced price for the replicated object or the work in the style of the original artist. The process of creation, or sale, of such a work therefore becomes a deception or fraud, and the increased value is dishonestly obtained, howsoever that might be addressed in the national law of the place of creation or sale. Absent the copyright protection afforded to modern works, a copy or replica is not itself necessarily 'illegal' if no fraud or deception was involved in its creation or sale, and for centuries artists have learned their trade by making and selling copies. Throughout history up to the nineteenth century, replicas were made of unique archetypes because demand far outstripped supply. The copies were not intended as forgeries, as such, because there was usually no attempt, by the replicating artist at least, to deceive the buyer into thinking they were purchasing the original. Ethical problems arise, however, when the replica status of an object is subsequently forgotten (or misrepresented), and it reemerges as an authentic original. The marble bust of *Clytie/Antonia* (AD *c.*40–50) in the British Museum is an example of the potential ethical ambiguities caused by replication. The work was originally believed to represent the mythological nymph Clytie; however, some modern scholars have reinterpreted her as the historical figure Antonia (36 BC–AD 38), daughter of Mark Antony, while others claim that it is an eighteenth-century replica. The current consensus is that this is a genuine Roman work, carved in antiquity, but heavily reworked in the eighteenth century to make it more erotic and attractive on the market at that time. Modern conservation ethics would decry the highly intrusive reworking of the piece in order to make it more appealing to the contemporary viewer.

The authentic status of many Old Masters is similarly called into question when scientific analysis reveals later remodellings and erasures or additions of features to an otherwise authentic work. In the art market, the Western collecting and connoisseurship tradition privileges the untouched original over the retouched or the replica, even if the replica is by the artist's hand as opposed to his studio. A recent example was the Frans Hals portrait of *Willem van Heythuysen* (1625), which exists in three extant versions. Of two of the versions, the 'Brussels' version was considered to be the original, until dendrochronology revealed the 'Rothschild' version to be the original of *c.*1638, and the 'Brussels' version to be an autographic replica of 1650. This revelation led to an increase in market value of the 'Rothschild' version from $527,460 in 2004 to $9.23 million in 2008, so the stakes for attribution, reattribution and the ethical conception of 'authenticity' can be high.

A further ethical question arises when works of art, known to be fakes and forgeries, nevertheless develop a curious cultural and resultant financial value of their own. After his suicide, forgeries of modern masters including Modigliani by Elmyr de Hory (1906–76) were exhibited in 1999 by Terrain Gallery, San Francisco, and typically sold for $20,000. If the aim of ethics is honesty and truth, then the encouragement of art forgeries by selling them in the legitimate open market is an ethical travesty. However there would be no question of 'legality' as they were sold for what they were, without deception or falsity.

The subject of ethics in the art world has given rise to a continuing and recently much energised debate, covering virtually every aspect of this very particular world, from art trading and sales practices to museum policies of acquisition, conservation, display and disposal, and even to how the art world treats the very objects that form its core. The only constant in these discussions is that there have been few constants, with attitudes changing in tune with developments in the societies of which the art world forms a part. Perhaps pivotal to these developments has been the growth of a more integrated global art economy, prompting the stirrings of a 'global view' on matters such as the protection of national and world heritage and a more transparent approach to sales, conservation and relationships in the art world in general. It would, however, be dangerous to overstate this trend; the art world will continue to throw up complex situations, giving rise to a range of different ethical responses, with the world's fragmented legal systems struggling as ever to keep up.

David Bellingham and Tom Christopherson

Bibliography

Bellingham, David, 'Frans Hals, Attribution and the Market' in Megan Aldrich and Jos Hackforth-Jones (eds), *Art and Authenticity*, Lund Humphries, 2012, ch.13, pp 22–36

Bellingham, David, 'Ethics and the Art Market' in Iain Robertson and Derrick Chong, *The Art Business*, Routledge, 2008, ch.10, pp 176–96

Bellingham, David, *The Underwater Heritage of the Riace Bronzes: Ethics and the Art Market in Ancient Rome* from the conference 'Art, Cultural Heritage and the Market: Ethical and Legal Issues', University of Maastricht, 15–16 March 2012

Charney, Noah, *Art Crime,* Palgrave Macmillan, 2015

Chamberlain, Kevin, *War and Cultural Heritage: A Commentary on the Hague Convention 1954 and Its Two Protocols*, Institute of Art and Law, 2004

Edson, Gary (ed.), *Museum Ethics*, Routledge, 2005

Friedman, Milton, 'The Social Responsibility of Business is to Increase Its Profits', *New York Times Magazine*, 13 September 1970

King, Elaine A., and Gail Levin (eds), *Ethics and the Visual Arts*, Skyhorse Publishing, Inc., 2013.

Marks, Peter, 'The Ethics of Art Dealing' in *International Journal of Cultural Property*, 1998, vol.7, no.1, pp 116–27

O'Keefe, Patrick and Lyndel Prott (eds), *Cultural Heritage Conventions and other Instruments*, Institute of Art and Law, 2011

O'Donnell, Nicholas, 'Detroit Institute of Arts and Motor City Bankruptcy: Deaccessioning Fact and Fiction, Hope and Reality', Sullivan & Worcester LLP Art Law report, 1 August 2013

Rosenbaum, Lee (CultureGrrl), 'Brandeis to "Deaccession" Its Entire Rose Art Museum', 26 January 2009, www.artsjournal.com

PUBLIC FUNDING AND
THE ART MARKET

The combination of 'public funding and the art market' may seem incongruent. Public funding is associated with the state (government) whereas the art market is seen as self-promoted for its relatively low level of regulation and private sector players. This private sector includes dealers and auction houses, as intermediaries, and individuals with high net worth as collectors. But several relationships between public funding and the art market can be identified. Firstly, an art market ecosystem relies on some degree of public funding for particular institutions, principally art schools and art museums, at different stages. Secondly, public funding is interpreted as direct subsidy thus undervaluing indirect subsidy. Thirdly, the nature of public funding assumes ideological choices by individual nations, including distinctions amongst liberal democracies and the benefit to the art markets from the emergence of nations operating forms of state-controlled capitalism.

An art market ecosystem relies both on artists producing works of art and on places to exhibit and house these works of art. Public funding can play a role in both cases by supporting institutions. For example, attendance at art school, such as an MFA degree programme, is viewed internationally as an important entry portal to developing a career as a contemporary artist. Relatively few established contemporary artists have not attended art school. A similar case can be made for a university education and an art history degree as typical prerequisites to be a director at a leading art museum. The terms 'museum quality' and 'masterpiece' are used by dealers and auction houses to promote works of the highest calibre. It is based on the view that the museum performs an idealised role as final repository of the most valued works of art made accessible to the general public. One way to endorse a collector's discernment is an invitation onto a museum or gallery's board of trustees; this may be followed by a collector's bequest of works to that institution's permanent collection. The nature of public funding devoted to art schools (which are often part of universities) and art museums is a political decision and remains a major preoccupation regarding public policy and the arts in liberal democracies.

The element of subsidy within public funding can exist in two ways. Direct subsidies are transfers of money (collected as taxes) via government departments or agencies (such as arts councils) to arts organisations or artists, while indirect subsidies are represented by government policy that influences relative prices or relative returns. The taxation system is a particular example of indirect subsidy that can influence the behaviour of private donors, foundations and business corporations. The state agrees not to collect the full taxes on income or testamentary estates devoted to civic or educational purposes, thus devolving this decision such that it is both individual and private.

Direct subsidies to the arts are a contested issue. There are many traditional arguments proffered in support of subsidies, primarily that the arts are considered a so-called merit good, having merit beyond private benefits; at the same time, the arts would be under-consumed, or under-produced, in a free market economy. It can be argued that the arts produce positive externalities in the form of public benefits – such as civilising society, enhancing national pride and engendering a collective identity – that outweigh private benefits. Furthermore, economic externalities from the arts, in helping to promote tourism and to attract businesses to expand local job opportunities, are considered spillover effects (that economists attempt to measure as a multiple of arts spending). Also, the equity argument holds that the arts should be made available to all, not least of all to citizens with low socio-demographic profiles. Thus the arts may have a social impact role in helping to address inequalities. Detractors of direct subsidies cite two main reasons: state paternalism and regressive taxation. A high degree of state paternalism is behind the merit good assumption that the state knows best. Public subsidy represents the state's effort to dictate popular taste, which is to say that if a cultural institution cannot please consumers and pay its way in a free market, then it has no economic justification, and if there is no economic justification, there can be no social justification. Some institutions, according to critics, wish to use the state's resources for their own purposes. Public subsidy endangers the autonomy of the arts by making artists and arts organisations dependent on government and thereby vulnerable to government control such as performance metrics. Arguably, public subsidy is a form of regressive taxation as it represents a net transfer of income from the poorer to the higher-income and educated classes. A similar case of regressive taxation is made in the case of state-controlled lotteries with some proceeds directed to the arts.

The nature of public funding assumes ideological choices by individual nations. If liberal democracies are represented by the US, UK, France, Germany and Italy, the rise of state-controlled capitalism includes China, Qatar and the United Arab Emirates (UAE). Indirect subsidies have been described as a key benefit of the taxation system in the US. As a young nation, the American ideals of freedom and individual initiative, built on a strong suspicion of central authority, underlay the formation of arts organisations in the US following the Civil War, as private and local organisations were managed like business corporations. There has been no large-scale and continuous tradition of direct subsidy by the government to support the arts and humanities in the US, where growing prosperity was the norm between the so-called Gilded Age (1865–1901) and the Wall Street Crash of 1929. During this period, following the end of the Civil War, great private fortunes were made, marked by the rise of the so-called robber barons and the making of America's extremely wealthy aristocratic families such as the Rothschilds, Vanderbilts, Astors, Rockefellers and Cabots. Some of the money that was amassed was spent on buying art from Europe and shipping these works to New York, Philadelphia and Boston. More importantly, the vast accumulation of private capital was used to create what are now considered leading museums, such as the Metropolitan Museum of Art, the Museum of Fine Arts, Boston, the Philadelphia Museum of Art, the Art Institute of Chicago, the Detroit Institute of Arts and the Cleveland Museum of Art. (The same phenomenon is evident in music with the formation of what emerged as the Big 5 symphony orchestras in the US in New York, Boston, Chicago, Philadelphia and Cleveland. These private institutions by the leading art museums were directly and self-consciously informed by European precedents, but with commitments to education encoded in their charters. The development of elite cultural institutions served as an extension of authority as part of a network of male, social, philanthropic and business venture for the emerging American establishment.

In Europe there is a longer cultural tradition with state patronage as an outgrowth of royal patronage and church commissions in maintaining a commitment to culture. In the UK, following the economic neoliberalism of Thatcherism, there has been a perceived move of the political centre to the right. The UK's welfare state response to supporting the arts via direct subsidy, following the end of the Second World War, has given way to a so-called mixed arts economy, one of plural funding. This means a gradual reduction in the relative level of direct subsidy with arts organisations seeking numerous different sources of funding to include self-generated revenue (admissions, publishing and merchandising), corporate sponsors and private donations from individuals. A return to a greater focus on philanthropy in the UK in the twenty-first century is a reminder that leading art museums established during the reign of Queen Victoria – such as the National Gallery, the Victoria and Albert Museum and Tate – also rely on the initiative of private patrons.

On the continent, France, Germany and Italy have adopted differing attitudes to culture and the state. Higher levels of public funding, as in continental Europe, relative to the US and UK, do not necessarily benefit the art market. With the formation of France's Fifth Republic in 1958, under Charles de Gaulle, André Malraux was appointed as the first Secretary of State for Cultural Affairs. Malraux promoted decentralisation, namely the development of *maisons de culture* in regional capitals. At the same time, during the 1960s, the French government was aware that Paris was losing its lustre and pre-eminence as the world's artistic capital. That there is much visible evidence to suggest that Paris matters most when it comes to arts and culture owes much to the presidency of Georges Pompidou, who went against the general principle of decentralisation, and immortalised himself by commissioning a museum of modern art. President Valéry Giscard d'Estaing pushed for the Musee d'Orsay; François Mitterrand is remembered as the president responsible for the *grands projets*, including La Defence, the Bibliothèque Nationale, L'Opera and the Louvre pyramid, which have been recognised as part of the architectural patronage of the state. Paris is considered one of the museum capitals of the world (with those devoted to single artists such as Bourdelle, Delacroix, Le Corbusier, Maillol, Moreau, Picasso and Rodin complementing other leading museum attractions). It represents a prime example of prestige arguments for state subsidy. On the other hand, the central role of Paris in the contemporary art market, as a site for artistic production and distribution, has been declining since the end of the Second World War, with the rise of New York and London.

The redrafting of the (then West) German constitution in 1949 made education and culture into *länder* (federal subdivisions) and local matters. This highly decentralised system was established as a means to deter the worst aspects of fervent nationalism. Post-unification Germany with its sixteen *länder* has local municipalities competing for civic stature via the arts, with each claiming to be the most cultural. One result of this competition is a widespread distribution of museums, orchestras, theatres and all kinds of arts activities throughout the nation. Berlin, with its affordable rents, emerged at the outset of the twenty-first century as a centre for artists. However, there appears to be less interest in developing the city as a site for the trade in contemporary art.

Many consider Italy one giant museum. Italy's cultural heritage, which includes the historical role of the Catholic Church, exists in situ and forms part of its inhabitants' daily experience. The lack of a mercantile revolution and growing secularisation during the three centuries between the sacking of Rome in 1527 (marking the end of the High Renaissance) and the Napoleonic Wars meant that the country was able to flourish as a gigantic cultural warehouse. Italy has to address unique cultural issues in managing what may be described as the largest open-air heritage site in the Western world. With conservation, restoration, and protection as paramount issues, it has adopted very strict export regulations regarding cultural property.

Outside of these liberal democracies are countries that operate a state-controlled capitalism, which means that a free market economy exists with a high level of state control. In the case of China, the state is the Communist Party of China, whereas absolute monarchs assume the role of the state in Qatar and the UAE. Moreover, unlike in liberal democracies, there is a lack of democratic accountability. In the case of China, the status of Hong Kong as a 'Special Administrative Region' (since the transfer of sovereignty from the UK in 1997) has been important to the art market. Hong Kong is now the third centre for trade across various art market sectors. The emergence of contemporary artists from China to the leading ranks of contemporary artists is also significant.

Both Qatar and the UAE have evolved since they were created in 1971 as independent nations, following the end of formal protectorate status by the UK and the complete British withdrawal from the Arab Gulf region. Both nations have sought to diversify their economic platform beyond natural resources by competing in the art market – Doha in Qatar and principally Abu Dhabi, Dubai and Sharjah in the UAE – particularly since the latter half of the 2000s. Both have started to become areas of increasing interest for elite art market players. This is evident in the location of auction houses (Christie's in Dubai and Sotheby's in Doha), art dealers (represented by art fairs such as Art Dubai and Abu Dhabi Art), biennials (Sharjah Biennial under the direction of Sheikha Hoor Al Qasimi since 2003) and new art museum buildings designed by 'starchitects'. This range of art market activity challenges some assumptions that the production of art is the starting point. Rather the focus is on the business and the impact of art on the economy. Qatar's position in the art market is dominated by the ruling Al-Thani family as leading collectors of art, including the purchase of numerous individual art works for sums in excess of $50 million during the past two decades. This includes Sheikha Al-Mayassa Al-Thani, who heads the state-run Qatar Museums (formerly Qatar Museums Authority). Signature buildings among Qatari museums include the I.M. Pei-designed Museum of Islamic Art, Mathaf, the Arab Museum of Modern Art by architect Jean-François Bodin, and the Jean Nouvel-designed National Museum of Qatar. Similarly, in the UAE there are art museum franchises on Saadiyat Island, principally the Frank Gehry-designed Guggenheim Abu Dhabi and the Jean Nouvel-designed Louvre Abu Dhabi as art museum partners. A certain sameness may be detected due to the homogenising force of globalisation.

Derrick Chong

Bibliography

Appignanesi, Lisa (ed.), *Culture and the State*, Institute of Contemporary Arts, 1984

Cowen, Tyler, *In Praise of Commercial Culture*, Harvard University Press, 1998

Cowen, Tyler, *How the United States Funds the Arts*, Endowment for the Arts, 2004

Cowen, Tyler, *Good and Plenty: the Creative Successes of American Arts Funding*, Princeton University Press, 2006

Dorian, Frederick, *Commitment to Culture: Art Patronage in Europe: Its Significance for America*, University of Pittsburgh Press, 1964

Steyerl, Hito, 'Is the Museum a Battlefield?', performance-lecture, Istanbul Biennial and Stedelijk Museum, 2012

ART MARKETS

ART MARKET SECTORS

It is a sobering thought that each one of the billions of art objects ever created is a unique commodity as far as the art market is concerned. In order to rationalise this unusual statistical conundrum, commercial galleries, dealers and collectors, auction houses and museums have developed categories based on the geographic origin, date, medium, content and style of the art. Whereas art history categorises these into periods, styles and genres, the market refers to them as sectors or segments.

The relationship between art history and the art market is a fascinating symbiosis, where the cultural (or symbolic) value attributed to art by art history both overlaps and differs from the financial value attributed by the market. In order to understand the dynamics of cultural and financial values today, it is essential to study the historical background of the relationship as it developed in the ancient Mediterranean world. In the last three centuries BC the Romano-Hellenistic art market developed simultaneously with art history. Both had their systems of categorising art objects, with the market tending to award as much value to precious metal vessels as to paintings and sculptures, particularly when acquired by military generals as war booty. The early Greco-Roman art histories on the other hand privileged what today we would refer to as the 'fine art' categories of painting and sculpture. They discussed these in terms of their aesthetic qualities, and divided them into genres based on content, such as portrait, still-life and landscape. Although little physical evidence survives, it is probable that the first public museums and private art collections followed these generic categorisations. Although the 'decorative arts' were discussed in terms of the financial value of their materials and craftsmanship, contemporary literary sources suggest that they were considered inferior in relation to the discourses surrounding 'fine art'. This hierarchical Classical legacy was rediscovered and resurrected during the Renaissance, and, as famously argued by John Berger (b.1926) in his book and TV series *Ways of Seeing* (1972), remains very much with us today, with our own persistent cultural and financial privileging of paintings and sculptures, both ancient and modern.

The two historical categorisations of art as 'fine' and 'decorative' have been further divided into sub-categories such as painting and sculpture, or furniture, glass and ceramics, for example. Yet further art-historical sub-divisions have focused on geographical origin and/or date, such as 'The Seventeenth-century Dutch School'. With the advent of Modernism, these categories became the '-isms' of the late nineteenth and twentieth centuries, such as impressionism, cubism, surrealism, Pop and postmodernism. These more recent '-isms' give primacy to stylistic categorisation and have been applied retrospectively to older artistic styles such as mannerism, Baroque, Rococo and neo-Classicism. This stylistic method of categorising art remains embedded in our educational culture, with the foundation modules of most art history courses still based on the geographical/date categories and '-isms', employing formal analysis to define and identify styles.

The art market has, in general, followed these art-historical categories in defining its own sectors. Thus commercial galleries tend to specialise in a particular geographical area, school of artists or stylistic period. This is true of traditional as well as contemporary art galleries, with both associating themselves with particular types of art, as well as organising special exhibitions based on solo or groups of artists, and sometimes themes. Since the new millennium, however, an increasing number of traditional galleries have begun to sell international contemporary art as a market response to the current boom in interest in the contemporary. This has also encouraged 'cross-collecting' of the art of different periods and types, and reflects a certain trend towards synchronic (or mixed-period) thematic displays of art as first appeared in the new curatorial strategies of gallery director Nicholas Serota (b.1946) at Tate Britain and Tate Modern in 2000.

In auction houses in the West, expert departments maintain the traditional art market sectors. These mirror art-historical categories with some interesting variations: antiquities; Old Masters; nineteenth-century; impressionist and modern; post-war and contemporary. Antiquities sales are limited to 'Western' antiquities, specifically Egyptian, Mesopotamian, Greek and

Roman. With globalisation, it is quite likely that other antiquity sectors from emerging markets such as China and Latin America will soon combine with these sales, and will include non-Western archaeological objects such as Chinese and Pre-Columbian grave goods. Although the turnover of this sector is minimal compared to the others, worth just 0.4 per cent of the Western auction market in 2015, sales results consistently outperform pre-sale estimates, indicating that this remains a profitable investment sector, with demand exceeding supply. There are, however, significant and serious ethical issues relating to the provenance of antiquities, including the illicit trade in illegally excavated archaeological objects together with the constant stream of antiquities looted from areas in conflict and in war zones. At the highest end of this market, the *Guennol Lioness*, a miniature limestone figure of an anthropomorphic lioness, sold at Sotheby's New York in 2007 for $75.16 million, tripling its upper estimate. This was due to a number of factors: its extreme antiquity (*c.*3000 BC); its rarity and uniqueness; its 'good provenance', said to have been found *c.*1930 near Baghdad by the famous British archaeologist Sir Leonard Woolley and its later acquisition by the Brooklyn Museum, who displayed it until its sale. Other types of antiquity that currently excel at auction are life-size marble statues of Classical goddesses, high-quality Roman Imperial portrait busts and rare bronzes. At the very low end of the market, reasonable-quality Greek and Roman coins can be purchased for a few hundred pounds.

Medieval art does not have its own auction sector, primarily because of the rarity, as well as the religious nature, of most of the objects, although there are a few commercial galleries that specialise in this category of art. Medieval manuscripts are a niche auction sector, usually sold alongside Renaissance books and manuscripts. Books of Hours, with their exquisite miniature paintings, are currently much sought after.

Old Master paintings cover a very broad period of art (*c.*1300–1800; artists born before 1760), and in this respect the sector differs markedly from the many divisions employed in the equivalent art-historical narrative. The reason for its breadth is the scarcity of high-quality works by famous names in the art-historical canon and therefore when a quality work by a renowned artist appears at auction, it attracts attention from across the world and thus sells for a record price. An interesting 'substitute' market has developed whereby serious collectors have created a kind of parallel market-oriented art history of lesser-known artists. The world record at auction for an Old Master painting was achieved in 2002 at Sotheby's London when *Massacre of the Innocents* (1611–12) by Peter Paul Rubens (1577–1640) sold for $65.27 million. The reasons for the high price included its recent rediscovery and reattribution led by a Sotheby's expert to Rubens, and the near-perfect condition of the painted surface. The sector title 'Old Masters' is considered by some to be a little old-fashioned – the term is rarely used in contemporary art history – and Sotheby's has currently rebranded its New York sales as 'Master Paintings' in order to appeal to younger collectors. The semantics of the term 'Old Masters' also signifies the necessary connoisseurship required to deal and to collect within the sector. An in-depth understanding of materials, replication, condition and authorship is required. Old Master drawings form an important, generally less expensive, niche sub-sector with its own sales and specialist dealers. The symbolic, and therefore financial, value of works not adjudged to be definitely by the hand of the artist is greatly reduced. In both academic art history and the art market there is a hierarchy of such values with works by the artist at the top, followed by 'attributed to', 'studio of', 'circle of', 'follower of', 'after' and 'in the style of.' Works in the latter two categories might be replicas or stylistic reflections of the artist painted at a much later date, and sell for comparatively low prices. 'Vedute' or 'view paintings' produced as souvenirs for eighteenth-century Grand Tourists are currently amongst the most commercial Old Masters, with their recognisable, non-religious, topographical views of Venice, Florence and Rome. The Old Master sector is worth just 5 per cent (2015) of the total Western fine art auction market, and like antiquities, works tend to hold their value over a longer period of time than some of the more recent sectors. High-end works tend to end up in public galleries, greatly subsidised by philanthropic contributions. In 2015 two major public collections, the Louvre, Paris and the Rijksmuseum, Amsterdam, combined their resources in a private treaty purchase by the Rothschild family of pendant portraits by Rembrandt (1606–69) for $180 million. The portraits will be shared between the two galleries.

Nineteenth-century paintings refers to Western nineteenth-century paintings in general, or those of a particular area or nation, including artists born between 1760 and 1860. This category often overlaps with other sectors; for example, outstanding nineteenth-century paintings by artists such as J.M.W. Turner (1775–1851) are often placed in Old Master sales because generally they will sell better there. Impressionist and post-impressionist paintings are excluded from the sector, appearing instead in impressionist and modern. This is an attractive and in many ways underrated sector, worth 5 per cent of the Western auction market (2015). The paintings are often of exceptional aesthetic quality and generally in better condition than equivalent Old Masters. However, they are less symbolically valuable because art history views many of them as derivative of earlier art. The most sought-after artists in the sector include those from the later French realist periods and Barbizon school such as Jean-Baptiste Corot (1796–1875) and Gustave Courbet (1819–77), together with the British Pre-Raphaelites. There are important national sub-sectors including British and Russian nineteenth-century paintings.

Impressionist and modern is arguably the most important and successful of all art market sectors in terms of long-term collecting and investment. It is the most valuable Western art market sector, worth 53 per cent (2015) of the total fine art auction market, with the modern works accounting for around 85 per cent of that total, and impressionist and post-impressionists at 15 per cent. The post-war and contemporary sector accounts for the second largest art market share at 36 per cent (2015), but that is arguably because it is undergoing a temporary bubble that may have peaked and therefore corrected its price levels. As with Old Masters, the impressionist and modern sector spans a broad period of art-historical activity covering highly important movements from impressionism and post-impressionism, through expressionism, cubism, surrealism and late Romanticism up to the Second World War. The sector performs particularly well because there is a good balance between supply and demand, and some of its key artists, including Claude Monet (1840–1926) and Pablo Picasso (1881–1973), were prolific producers. Their works commanded top prices during their lifetimes, and have continued to increase in symbolic and financial value, often exponentially. The sector sits on the cusp of tradition and modernity, and thus attracts a wide range of collectors, both young and old. The Picasso collector is able to obtain works ranging from his rare early twentieth-century figurative portraits to cubist paintings and the many classic modern works of his maturity. The Paris dealer

Paul Durand-Ruel (1831–1922) pioneered the process of marketing artists both locally and internationally, and he successfully exported impressionist and post-impressionist works to London and New York. Durand-Ruel's legacy is demonstrated by the continuing international demand for these artists in the twentieth century, which reached a peak in the 1980s with the Japanese passion for purchasing, at record prices, works by Monet, Pierre-Auguste Renoir (1841–1919) and Vincent Van Gogh (1853–90). The success of impressionism is unabated. The auction record is currently held by one of the 1919 Monet series *Nymphéas* (Water-lilies), which sold for $53.93 million at Christie's London in June 2008. The post-impressionist painting by Paul Gauguin (1848–1903) *Nafea Faa Ipoipo* (When Will You Marry?) was the world's most expensive work of art in 2015, selling for a purported $300 million, possibly to the Qatari royal family. Classic modern paintings are also within the world's top ten most expensive art works, with Picasso's *Les Femmes d'Alger (Version O)* (1955) selling for $179.3 million in 2015, followed by a *Reclining Nude* (1917–18) by Amadeo Modigliani (1884–1920), which sold for $170.4 million at Christie's, New York in 2015. It is significant in terms of the current fashion for cross-collecting that Liu Yiqian (b.1963), the Chinese billionaire buyer of the Modigliani, is better known as a collector of antique Chinese and Tibetan art.

The sale of the aforementioned Picasso was in a Christie's sale entitled *Looking Forward to the Past*. The sale marked a refreshing break from the parameters of traditional art market sectors by including just 33 top works by impressionist, modern as well as post-war and contemporary living artists, ranging from Monet and René Magritte (1898–1967), through to Andy Warhol (1928–87) and Peter Doig (b.1959). It remains to be seen whether impressionist to contemporary becomes a single new sector.

The post-war art market sector (artists born in the period 1920–45) is worth 25 per cent, whilst contemporary (artists born from 1946 onwards) is worth 11 per cent. The exponential growth of the contemporary art market since the new millennium is due to a number of cultural and financial factors. The growing national and international fame of the Young British Artists (YBAs) in the 1990s to early 2000s was boosted by the high-profile public display and marketing savvy of Charles Saatchi (b.1943). The *Sensation* exhibition in 1997 of 110 works from Saatchi's collection at the traditionally conservative Royal Academy prompted extreme reactions from press and public, leading to high media exposure of the YBAs to a much broader national and international public. The paintings and installations of Damien Hirst (b.1965) in particular became much sought after by a new generation of wealthy young collectors, themselves made rich by the financial boom of the early 2000s. In the footsteps of the Old Masters before them, Hirst, Jeff Koons (b.1955) and Takashi Murakami (b.1962) created workshops employing dozens of young artists in order to maintain a prolific supply of works to answer consumer demand for their post modern 'Pop art' styles. These high-end contemporaries, together with older-generation blue-chip living artists such as Gerhard Richter (b.1932), have led the way in the current boom in art collecting in this field. These individuals also demonstrated the importance of self-promotion for the success of the contemporary artist, who needs to become a commercial 'brand' in order to succeed in the competitive global art world. All of them sell less expensive multiples through retail outlets, and have co-branded themselves with other luxury commodities such as Louis Vuitton haute couture.

Confidence in the contemporary sector is underwritten by the increase in popularity of modern and contemporary art museums. Visitor numbers to these public institutions, however, rising since the turn of the millennium, appear to have peaked, with declining footfall since 2012. Likewise, the turnover for contemporary art at auction in 2015 showed a marked decline from the previous year. Commercial galleries and dealers in international contemporary art are also reporting a slowdown. There are a few exceptions with some record prices continuing to be broken, with Jeff Koons selling his *Balloon Dog (Orange)* at Christie's New York in 2013 for $58.4 million, whilst Gerhard Richter's *Abstraktes Bild* (1986) sold for $40 million at Sotheby's, London in 2015. These records relate arguably to high-end investment, as opposed to what is actually happening in contemporary artistic culture, where younger artists are constantly emerging across the globe but remain unexposed in the international market. At the same time, art market commentators report that collectors are turning to less volatile long-term investment sectors, such as Old Masters. Significantly, Old Master public galleries have experienced record visitor numbers since 2012, with visitor figures for the National Gallery, London reaching over 6 million in 2013, an increase of 14 per cent on the previous year. The Louvre, Paris and the Metropolitan Museum, New York have seen similar rises. In response to these cultural and market developments, some auction houses have begun to deliberately mix periods and genres, with Christie's presenting sales of high-end art from different sectors, and the French auction house Artcurial selling mixed genres in its Hong Kong sales.

Since the new millennium non-Western sectors have developed exponentially alongside the Western post-war and contemporary areas. However, whereas the latter sector grew primarily for reasons of fashion, non-Western sectors developed as a by-product of emerging economies. The BRICS nations (Brazil, Russia, India, China and South Africa) now account for 20 per cent of the world's gross product. They also make up over 40 per cent of the world's population. This combination of increased wealth and people has led to a massive increase in both new billionaires and the middle classes. The conspicuous purchase and display of art has become the prime symbol of this newly acquired wealth. Russia, China, Brazil and Mexico now actively 'buy back' their cultural heritage, leading to the increasingly high profile of pre-revolutionary art sectors in the first two of these nations. Chinese decorative art and antiques, together with Chinese painting and calligraphy, have proved the most consistently successful sectors, boosted by the creation of many new Chinese museums, each building its collection with acquisitions from the art market. Chinese and Indian contemporary areas performed very well until the start of global recession in 2007–8. These emerging sectors tend to form unsustainable bubbles, especially when their contemporary art fetches high prices at primary auction sales but is unvalidated by an established commercial or public gallery sector. For example, the work of contemporary Indian artists Subodh Gupta (b.1964) and Bharti Kher (b.1969) has successfully bridged the gap between their home country, with its virtual absence of public sector validating museums, and the West, where their works have not only been sold at auction on the primary market, but have also been validated by their display in Tate Modern and Museum of Modern Art, New York, as well as in public spaces. Some Chinese contemporary art appears in Western auctions, whereas Chinese antiquities and Old Masters continue to be sold separately. The current record for a Chinese Old Master is $61.3 million for a scroll painting of 1350 by Wang Meng (1308–85). This sold at the Poly auction house in 2011. More recently, the so-called MINT nations (Mexico, Indonesia, Nigeria and Turkey) have developed emerging art market sectors, although they, like the BRICS, tend to suffer from the absence of a historically established art market with validating public and quasi-public galleries.

Art market sectors will continue to evolve in response to changes in the global cultural landscape, with auction houses constantly seeking out new markets by theming sales around new collecting fashions, such as, in 2015, Latin-American art (including Cuban), post-war Italian art, Franco-Chinese art or South Korean monochrome painting. Similarly established Western visual culture sectors outside of the traditional market for fine and decorative art have begun to establish themselves as growing art market areas. These include twentieth- and twenty-first-century design, the modern equivalent of decorative art, which produced a 2014 auction turnover of €314 million. In the future, with increasing globalisation of artistic production and the recent growth in cross-collecting, it is not difficult to imagine strong new sectors developing which ignore both chronological and national boundaries, themed by similarity of subject, function or media.

David Bellingham

Bibliography

Berger, John, *Ways of Seeing*, Penguin, 2008, vol.1

'The Contemporary Art Market: The Artprice Annual Report 2015', imgpublic. artpublic.com

McAndrew, Clare, *TEFAF Maastricht Art Market Report 2015*, European Fine Art Foundation, 2015

Pollitt, Jerome Jordan, *The Art of Ancient Greece: Sources and Documents.*, Cambridge University Press, 1990

Velthuis, Olav, and Stefano Baia Curioni (eds), *Cosmopolitan Canvases: the Globalization of Markets for Contemporary Art*, Oxford University Press, 2015

THE CONTEMPORARY PHOTOGRAPHY MARKET

Photography is a relatively recent addition to the market for international contemporary art. Invented in 1839, in the early years it served to record events and people. This is evident in the portraits of early photographers such as Julia Margaret Cameron (1815–79). If it had claims to 'high art' at all, it drew on many of the attributes and qualities of painting. As a result of the determined, combined efforts on the part of many key art market institutions throughout its development, prices for contemporary photography today can be as much as $4 million.

The key to understanding the market for contemporary photography today is the arduous journey that photography has undergone to earn the art establishment's validation as a respected art form. This artistic struggle is exacerbated by the absence in the case of photographs of the key art market attribute: rarity. Singularity is one of the essential building blocks in the art market edifice. Photography, by its very nature, is a process of mechanical reproduction, which was originally conceived as a means of enabling the production of identical, multiple images. Overcoming the twin pitfalls, a perception of artistic deficit and the absence of scarcity, has required the joint and extensive efforts of both the art world's and art market's important players. The shift in awareness within the art world's ecosystem has been a complex and arduous one.

Despite the public's familiarity with the medium of photography, via print media, advertising and wide-scale amateur practice, it was not until the mid-twentieth century that the appearance of photography in the context of the museum began to widen appreciably. The validation of photography through these accepted bastions of symbolic cultural capital has swiftly constructed the foundations on which a market can thrive. The Museum of Modern Art in New York is perhaps the most significant vehicle in the validation of photography as an art form; it had established a dedicated photography department as early as 1942. The museum is as enthusiastic today as it was adventurous in the beginning for endorsing the validity of photography as an integral part of contemporary art. It has sought to scupper the impression that photography is in some way the poor cousin of a grand relation.

The Getty Museum in California has, more recently, played an equally strident role in the promotion of art photography. In 1983, for instance, it acquired three major photographic collections for the substantial sum of $20 million, which included the greatly respected Jammes Collection, Crane Collection and Wagstaff Collections, endowing the Getty with a wealth of predominantly modern and nineteenth-century masterworks. The purchase signalled a long-term commitment to photography, which did much to bolster art market confidence.

The market was relatively slow to grasp the potential of photography as a commodity. A groundbreaking 1971 London sale at Sotheby's, dedicated solely to the medium, is considered to be the start of the contemporary art market for photography. The auction led to the establishment of a dedicated department of photography at Sotheby's in 1977. The other leading auction houses, Phillips and Christie's, followed suit. In the 1990s it became evident standard practice that contemporary photography was included auctions devoted to international contemporary art. This critical development enabled photography to be perceived, and valued, as an art form on a par with paintings and sculpture. To support this claim, artists of the stature of Cindy Sherman (b.1954) and Andreas Gursky (b.1955) attained prices the equivalent of the most expensive international contemporary art. The current standing record for a photograph sold at auction was set in 2011 by Andreas Gursky's *Rhein II* (1999), which sold for $4.34 million. The average price level of photography has substantially increased on the back of these record sales.

The photography market began a rapid cycle of growth, experiencing a dramatic increase of 285 per cent between 1993 and 2008, with auction prices rising by 83 per cent between 1998 and 2008. The contemporary photography market (including artists born after 1940) today comprises a quarter of the auction market for international photography. The modern market (photographers born between 1890 and 1940) comprises half the market, and the nineteenth-century sector the remaining quarter. These figures underplay the significant market stature of the contemporary photography sub-sector. They represent only the results from dedicated photography auctions and do not include the significantly higher-priced contemporary photographs that are successfully sold via international contemporary art auctions. In 2005 only a single photograph managed to break the $1 million price barrier at auction, but since that date a total of 92 photographs have sold above $1 million. A total of 87 per cent of these have been contemporary photographs.

Significant American dealers in photography such as Harry Lunn (b.1934) pioneered the practice of selling work as part of an edition. A strict condition of this practice is that the dealer guarantees that the artist will limit the number of prints produced from a particular image to an explicitly stated maximum number. Lunn represented well-regarded photographers such as Ansel Adams (1902–84) and Edward Weston (1886–1958), both of whom observed, conscientiously, the practice of producing a limited edition. Photography, in a sense, managed intelligently to create self-imposed, artificial rarity through the practice of authorising a limited edition. The notion of creating an artificially constrained series of identical images is widespread in the art world. It has provided a solution to the absence of rarity in this market and it has successfully acted as a brake to excess supply, both of which, left unaddressed, radically depress value.

Photography has, since the 1990s, been promoted and represented by a significant number of general commercial contemporary galleries internationally. The medium had been historically represented via a smaller network of specialist photography galleries. The presence of photography in the contemporary art marketplace (at galleries, art fairs, etc.) has exposed it to a wider collector base and to one that is more extravagant. In that sense the secondary (dealer) market's strategy of engaging a more high-profile, monied collector base has successfully dovetailed with the auction houses' identical efforts, effectively expanding the market for contemporary photography well beyond its historical walls.

Photographers have themselves made important efforts in building the market for their work. Major technological advancements have enabled photographers to create large-scale, high-impact colour images, keeping pace with today's international contemporary art works, and sitting beside increasingly large-scale global museum and gallery spaces. The success of this formula is evidenced via the combined efforts, and commercial rewards, of the group of photographers often referred to as the Düsseldorf School of Photography (including Andreas Gursky, Candida Hofer (b.1944), Thomas Struth (b.1954) and Thomas Ruff (b.1958)), who studied under the influential direction of Bernd and Hiller Becher in the 1970s.

In terms of the new directions that contemporary photography has taken, the more recently developing sub-sectors of fashion and documentary photography have seen much commercial growth largely owing to the support and marketing efforts of the major auction houses, as well as the very familiar presence of these images in magazines, advertising and newspapers. Photography has also taken on an important documentation role in conjunction with the leading growth sub-sectors of performance and installation art. Photographic representations of these more challenging, ethereal works have become a practical means of commodifying these works for the collector. Photographic film stills taken from art video clips perform a similar function. A great deal of artistic innovation and growth in the photography market has developed at a rapid pace via many of the financial growth hubs of key emerging, non-Western art markets such as China and the Middle East. Chinese contemporary photographers such as Wang Qinsong (b.1966) and Zhang Huan (b.1965), as well as leading Middle Eastern photographers such as Shirin Neshat (b.1957) and Walid Raad (b.1967), have become established names in the international contemporary art scene.

The even more recent twenty-first-century growth of digital photography has raised a number of artistic and conservation concerns. Such issues include the long-term stability and longevity of digital prints, with insufficient time having yet passed to establish the long-term appreciation of these works. The vast array of technological techniques available to manipulate and alter photographic images has also been the subject of much debate in photography circles, purists believing that this increasing practice erodes the established documentary role historically played by photography.

Photography art fairs have also played a vital role in the growth, and widespread promotion of the international photography market. The most important date in the international photography market calendar is the *Paris Photo* art fair, held annually in Paris since 1996, which, significantly, moved its venue to the prestigious Grand Palais in 2011. The fair attracts major global contemporary galleries, including Gagosian, David Zwirner and Pace. AIPAD (Association of International Photography Art Dealers) is the major US-based fair, held in New York since 1980. A remarkable number of important new fairs dedicated solely to photography, including Photo London, Photo Shanghai, Photo Basel and Photo San Francisco (2017), were launched in 2014 and 2015, signalling a new wave of global interest and market growth in what is increasingly seen to be a prime collecting sub-sector.

Photography's relatively modest prices within the international contemporary art sector are a factor which makes photography a highly popular addition within the rapidly growing online art market. Photography's universal familiarity and ease of display in the online environment are providing important commercial opportunities to engage an innovative global body of newly engaged collectors.

Jeffrey Boloten

Bibliography

www.arttactic.com

www.artprice.com

Campany, David, *Art and Photography*, Phaidon Press, 2003

Cotton, Charlotte, *The Photograph as Contemporary Art*, Thames & Hudson, 2014

Durden, Mark, *Photography Today: A History of Contemporary Photography*, Phaidon, 2014

Newhall, Beaumont, *The History of Photography: From 1839 to the Present*, Secker & Warburg, 1982

Gapper, John, 'How Annie Got Shot', *Financial Times Magazine*, 22 October 2010

Hacking, Juliet (ed.), *Photograph: The Whole Story*, Thames & Hudson, 2012

Soutter, Lucy, *Why Art Photography?*, Routledge, 2013

DESIGN ART AND ITS MARKETS

Most twentieth-century and contemporary design comprises mass produced items of everyday use, which do not generally have value in the international art market. Objects that do sell at auction, and through dealers and galleries, tend to be by well-known designers and are frequently unique pieces, or those produced in limited numbers which attract collectors because of their rarity, provenance and/or cultural significance. Overall, however, the market for design is more limited than that for modern and contemporary art. In 2000 the term Design Art (also referred to as DesignArt, designart and design-art) was coined in 2000 by Alexander Payne, director of design at Phillips de Pury & Co., who observed that some designers experimented with materials and form to the extent that the boundaries between art and design were blurred. Payne sensed that these works opened up new possibilities in terms of the market and, accordingly, Phillips de Pury retitled its New York sales of twentieth-century design 'Design Art'; as the new millennium unfolded, these auctions came to include more contemporary pieces by designers such as Ron Arad (b.1951), Marc Newson (b.1963) and Zaha Hadid (1950–2016).

The reclassification of sales is not an unusual practice within the auction world – it is an obvious way to revitalise the market and to differentiate one house from its competitors. In this case, however, the use of the term Design Art was not limited to Phillips but permeated the wider design network of dealers, collectors and manufacturers; indeed, in 2007 a new fair, launched to coincide with Frieze in London, was titled DesignArt London. Articles discussing Design Art appeared in the press during the 2000s, and a small number of publications explored the phenomenon, notably Sophie Lovell's *Limited Edition, Prototypes, One-Offs and Design Art Furniture* of 2009. (Significantly, Bruno Munari's *Design as Art*, first published in 1966, was reprinted in 2008.) Exhibitions on Design Art included *Design High* at the Louise Blouin Foundation and *Telling Tales: Fantasy and Fear in Contemporary Design* at the Victoria and Albert Museum, both staged in 2009.

Design Art described a small number of objects, predominantly furniture, which sought to sidestep mass manufacture and the conventional retail trade to adopt creative and commercial practices more usually associated with the art world. Thus, Design Art objects were frequently made using materials and hand or technologically advanced processes that rendered quantity production difficult and/or prohibitively expensive. Instead, the pieces were produced as limited editions (of 8, 10 or 12 for example), usually accompanied by one or more artist's proofs and prototypes – methods and language that mimic those used in the art world for sculptures, prints and photographs. This type of production was made possible by the presence of dealers who assisted the designers practically (and often financially) to realise their projects, which became more exclusive products sold in their galleries rather than in conventional retail outlets. The approach was pioneered by figures such as David Gill, who founded his London gallery in 1986 and offered limited editions from 1989; Didier Krzentowski, who opened Galerie Kreo in Paris in 1992; and Ron Arad, who opened his One-Off Gallery in London in 1982. They were followed by galleries such as Established and Sons (2005), Carpenters Workshop Gallery (2006), Libby Sellers (2007) in London, and others in New York and elsewhere. Moreover, Malletts, the renowned dealer in antiques, launched Meta in 2008 – a project that aligned contemporary designers with skilled craftspeople to create limited-edition items, most notably Tord Boontje's *Fig Leaf* wardrobe. These ventures were further supported by the incorporation of design into art fairs such as Design Miami in 2005.

Design Art objects were not only pieces which explored alternative ways of making and selling design but were often works in which aesthetic and conceptual concerns were privileged over practicality (usually regarded as the primary purpose of design): in Design Art, form follows idea rather than function. Thus, objects assumed the status of sculpture – they were not necessarily to be used, but to be contemplated and understood in the same manner as a work of art. One consequence of this was that some galleries traditionally associated with fine art began to involve themselves with design: Gagosian brought the designer Marc Newson into its stable, Timothy Taylor took on Ron Arad, and Ross Lovegrove (b.1958) and Stuart Haygarth (b.1966) were taken up by the Haunch of Venison. At the same time, the term Design Art was being used to describe tendencies within fine art practice to explore and integrate elements from architecture and design. Publications by Alex Coles investigated the historical and ongoing dialogue between artists and the design world, examining twentieth-century precedents and the work of contemporary figures such as Franz West (1947–2012) and Jorge Pardo (b.1963). Barbara Bloemink and Joseph Cunningham's *Design Does Not Equal Art* (2004) considered similar territory, while the Düsseldorf exhibition *U.F.O. Blurring the Boundaries between Art and Design* in 2009 included works by both artists and designers and thus interrogated the interface between the two disciplines.

And yet, almost as quickly as it had entered both the art and the design worlds, the label Design Art vanished. By 2008, Payne had distanced himself from the term and the sales at Phillips were retitled simply 'Design', including those held in the London sale room which opened in that year. In 2009, the DesignArt London fair was renamed Pavilion of Art and Design (PAD). Whilst the contentious debate about the boundaries between art and design remains ongoing (and, indeed, has a long history), a title that seemed to encapsulate the porous nature of those boundaries (and perhaps even encouraged cross-border activity) was abandoned within a decade. During its brief reign, Design Art provoked considerable debate within the design community, but the discussion centred not only on the name but also on the objects that fell into its remit.

There seems little doubt that there was a ready market for Design Art in the early 2000s. Since the affluent 1980s (the 'design decade'), when furniture and other objects became crucial signifiers of wealth, status and lifestyle, there had been a steady rise in design consciousness, fuelled by the media through magazines and television make-over programmes. The resultant widespread consumption of objects was facilitated by increased accessibility through high street brands which moved into the home furnishings market, by the global expansion of Swedish furniture store Ikea, and by the reproduction of so-called 'design classics' by companies such as Knoll and Vitra. In such a climate, and in such a buoyant economy, wealthy individuals sought to distinguish themselves by furnishing their homes with more exclusive objects – the type offered by limited-edition Design Art. Contemporary art collectors in particular were prepared to pay a premium for pieces that would complement their fine art acquisitions and Design Art objects, hovering in the visual and intellectual no-man's land between art and design, fitted the bill perfectly. The art world, which thrives on the unique and the rare (enabling higher prices to be charged), capitalised on this, as did the new network of design galleries and fairs. It is not surprising, therefore, that it was those within the commercial art world who tended to favour the term and who also sought to promote Design Art as a new phenomenon. Critics of Design Art, on the other hand, regarded it as being nothing more than a marketing ploy used to inflate prices and entice wealthy collectors from the booming contemporary art market into new territory.

The idea, however, that a designed object can be about more than functionality is not in itself new: religious items, or those associated with royalty, are obvious examples of works that are highly charged with symbolic meanings. Earlier movements such as art nouveau had also sought to imbue practical objects with narrative. Indeed, throughout history, unique or limited numbers of objects have been made, frequently to commission, and the long and continuing tradition of handcraftsmanship has perpetuated this model of production. Overall, Design Art seemed to offer little that was actually new in terms of the production–consumption cycle, or in terms of ascribing meaning to functional items. One should perhaps view Design Art instead as a perpetuation of the reaction (evident from the 1960s) to the modernist insistence on rationality, functionality and mass production as the sole determinants of design, and as resistance to its belief that objects should be universal – that they should be appropriate to all people, in all contexts, and at all times. As earlier dissenters from the modernist creed, Design Art protagonists asserted the designer's right to creative freedom to explore innovative forms, materials and processes without the constraints of mass manufacture. They also reaffirmed that there is a plurality of markets for design, not one, and that different consumers seek different values in their objects and that these are not always limited to functionality.

A criticism of Design Art that arose from these considerations was that it led to the creation of eye-catching and flamboyant designs for an exclusive minority; that it had no impact on the sort of design with which most people engage on a daily basis or with some of the wider issues and problems that design should address. However, it has also been suggested that ambitious young designers such as Marc Newson used limited-edition designs such as the *Lockheed Lounge Chair* (1986) to build a media profile that would gain attention and lead to commissions within the mainstream industrial sector. Whilst it is undeniable that it was only available to the wealthy few, one could also argue that Design Art raised important questions about the purpose and meaning of objects, and our relationship to them, which have implications for large-scale production. Limited editions have less of an environmental impact than mass-manufactured goods and, because of their high monetary value, they are less likely to be thrown away than an inexpensive item from Ikea, for example. Accordingly, the durability of Design Art pieces can be regarded as a positive in an age of over-production, over-consumption and diminution of scarce resources.

Another notable concern of the term Design Art was the implication that design could not be valued on its own terms but needed the crutch of art to be taken seriously. Design and the decorative arts have long been considered the poor relations of painting and sculpture and the term was possibly seen to reinforce this hierarchical prejudice. This may explain a reluctance among designers themselves to embrace the term or to have their practice pigeon-holed as either art or design or both. There was also a certain reticence to engage critically with Design Art in academic circles, with most commentary emanating from art market reportage and the pens of journalists. Perhaps because Design Art emerged (or was appropriated by) the commercial art world, the issues and questions that it raised about design practice tended to be shunned by design historians traditionally hostile to the market. However, scholars such as Alex Coles and Gareth Williams have provided more sustained and contextualised accounts of Design Art, as part of a wider discussion on the relationship between art, design and craft, and no doubt a more reflective and critical discourse will emerge as a historical perspective develops.

Design Art pieces continue to be sold at auction but, since the term has been abandoned and prices have flattened following the economic crash of 2008, their presence in sales is less conspicuous overall; mid-century Italian and French furniture and lighting, together with examples of Scandinavian design, dominate at Phillips, for example. Marc Newson's aluminium *Lockheed Lounge Chair*, has arguably remained the success story of the market for Design Art. It sold at Christie's for $105,000 when the phenomenon was in its infancy in 2000, but it made $968,000 when it was sold at Sotheby's in New York in June 2006 – the highest price reached at auction for a work by a living designer. Despite the recession, the edition retained its value and in April 2015 the *Lockheed Lounge Chair* surpassed its own record when another example sold for $3.16 million at Phillips in London (this figure remains the auction record for a living designer). The work has remained significant not only because of its comparative rarity (only ten examples plus four artist proofs and one prototype were made) but also because the chair's seductively fluid form and finely crafted tactile surface, inspired by aircraft, had great influence on the neo-organic vocabulary for design which emerged in the 1990s. The chair thus has wider cultural implications beyond its Design Art status.

By contrast, the market for furniture by Zaha Hadid, another key figure in Design Art, has floundered. In April 2005, Established and Sons sold a prototype polyurethane *Aqua* dining table, one of her most iconic works, for $59,330. Eight months later, the same table was sold by Phillips de Pury in New York for $296,000. Since then, the table has struggled in the marketplace. An example from the edition of 12 failed to sell at Sotheby's in London in 2008 against an estimate of $156,800–$229,200; the same piece sold in 2011 for only $80,270. In May 2015, number 4 in the edition, estimated at $56,400 to $84,600, did not find a buyer at Phillips in London. One factor in this market decline may be the overscaled nature of Hadid's furniture, which is often seen as reduced versions of her architecture and therefore inappropriate for the domestic interior, just as the materials are often impractical.

Furniture by Ron Arad appears regularly on the art market as his output is substantially greater than that of either Newson or Hadid. Several of his distinctive *Big Easy Volume 2* armchairs, for example, have been sold globally. In 1998, prior to the Design Art bubble, the chair was estimated at $6,800–$9,080 at Artcurial in Paris, but failed to sell. By contrast, in the 2000s, examples reached between $48,800 and $54,450. Prices dipped slightly thereafter, but in October 2015 Artcurial held the first sale of its kind dedicated to the work of a single contemporary designer and a *Big Easy Volume 2* sold for $85,100. The auction house credited Arad with inventing the Design Art concept by producing works that could be viewed equally as sculpture and furniture; as such, he was felt to be the only contemporary designer on the market who could sustain a solo sale that would appeal equally to art and design collectors. All 20 lots sold in 35 minutes for $1,960,380, double the sale estimate, with Arad's *Restless* bookshelf (2007) selling for €423,920, a world record for the designer.

Despite an overall decline in the Design Art market and the abandonment of the name, material and conceptual experimentation remain vital aspects of contemporary design practice, although the work represents now (as in the 2000s) a small percentage of total output and is aimed at a limited number of consumers. The widening network of galleries, dealers and other platforms which Design Art generated continues to nurture creative freedom, and to release designers from the economic necessity of working for a saturated mass market with all its financial and marketing constraints. One might argue that the Design Art network permitted the creation of works that might not otherwise have seen the light of day and that this remains the case today. Further, the intense media debate surrounding the name Design Art, and the high prices of the works that fell under its umbrella, raised the profile of design, highlighting the breadth of approaches within the discipline. It is to be hoped that now the hype has subsided, and the inflated prices have stabilised, a more critical engagement with the meaning of design and its interface with art can move beyond concern with a mere name.

Lis Darby

Bibliography

Bloemink, Barbara and Joseph Cunningham, *Design Does Not Equal Art: Functional Objects from Donald Judd to Rachel Whiteread,* Merrell, in association with Cooper-Hewitt National Design Museum, 2004

Coles, Alex, *DesignArt: On Art's Romance with Design*, Tate Publishing, 2005

Coles, Alex, *Design and Art: Documents of Contemporary Art*, Whitechapel Art Gallery and MIT Press, 2007

Coles, Alex, 'Designart: A Symptom of Noughties Excess or a Model of Dynamic Interdisciplinary Practice', *Art Monthly,* 334, 2010, pp 7–10

Hage, Rabin and Karen Ryan, 'The Great DesignArt Debate', *Financial Times*, 11 April 2008

Lindemann, Adam, *Collecting Design*, Taschen, 2010

Lovell, Sophie, *Limited Edition, Prototypes, One-Offs and Design Art Furniture*, BirkhäuserVerlag AG, 2009

Rappolt, Mark, 'What Is Design Art?' *Art Review*, December 2009, pp 88–9

Rawsthorn, Alice, 'Whatever "Design-art" Is, It's Thriving', *New York Times*, 20 May 2008

Sellers, Libby, 'Why What How: Collecting Design in a Contemporary Market', HSBC Private Bank, 2010

Williams, Gareth, *Telling Tales: Fantasy and Fear in Contemporary Design*, V&A Publishing, 2009

EMERGING MARKETS

The linear 'advance' of culture is, arguably, a Western, post-Renaissance concept. It is one that globalists adhere to, believing that all peoples, cultures and civilisations ultimately speak a common language and simultaneously see the world, its current state and future development, in the same way. Cultural homogeneity is a natural response to a world dominated economically and politically by the United States. America values individualism (abstract expressionism) and enamelled beauty (Pop art) and both these conditions have infiltrated the art and cultures of emerging markets.

The nations that justify inclusion under the sobriquet of emerging markets broadly conform to those that are recently economically vital. So, the countries that comprise the acronyms and economic groupings: BRIC (Brazil, Russia, India, China), MINT (Mexico, Indonesia, Nigeria, Turkey), CIVETS (Colombia, Indonesia, Vietnam, Egypt, Turkey, South Africa) and MAVINS (Mexico, Australia, Vietnam, Indonesia, Nigeria, South Africa), are broadly considered in this survey of art markets, but divided according to their continental, cultural allegiances, which have been highlighted. Brazil, Mexico and Columbia (BMC) are considered under the term South America. Persia, Turkey and Pakistan are considered as separate entities that share a common Persianate/Islamic culture. Iran and Pakistan, exceptionally, are unrepresented in the four economic acronyms, but are culturally significant enough to be included in a study of emerging art markets. India and China are examined independently of themselves and other states. Indonesia, Thailand, Vietnam and the Philippines convoke under the heading South East Asia. Indonesia is nominated their representative because of its size and influence.

China is used as the measure of emerging art market effectiveness. It is the regional common denominator. In the period from the 1979 economic reforms instigated by paramount leader Deng Xiaoping (1904–97) to the acquisition of masterpieces by Chinese collectors like Wang Wei and Liu Yiqian in the second decade of the twenty-first century, Chinese works of art have achieved comparable prices and received as much worldwide approbation as Western fine art and antiques. The reason for this lies not in the efficiency of China's national art market, which is both recently reconstituted and unpredictable, but in the febrile nature of the buyers, both foreign and Chinese, in the first extended flush of wealth and excitement, aligned to the universally and historically high regard in which Chinese culture is held. Before 2007 no one in the art world believed that a Chinese contemporary oil painting would sell for over a million dollars. And yet that is what happened to the works of the group of five charmed Political Pop artists. The painting, *Family Portrait* (1994), by its unelected leader, Zhang Xiaogang (b.1958), made nearly $5 million at Sotheby's, New York in 2007. A year later in Hong Kong, a similar picture, *Bloodline: The Big Family No.3* (1995), attained a slightly higher price, and six years later this picture sold again in Hong Kong for $9.2 million. In 1998, at the inaugural overseas auction of the work of this avant-garde at Christie's in London, a pendant portrait by the artist made a mere $7,580. Another member of the loosely affiliated group, Yue Minjun (b.1962), went on to achieve comparable success to Zhang Xiaogang, selling two works for $16,571 and $17,324 at the same auction. The subsequent explosion in the value of this art was driven by excitable American collectors in search of a zeitgeist, succoured by able marketeers. The auction in Hong Kong of works grouped under the title of the Estella Collection in 2008 is the paramount example of this trend.

The eruption in the value of historic Chinese decorative works of art is a very different phenomenon. The price of these objects is driven by Chinese collectors, motivated primarily by a nationalist instinct, but also, and increasingly as knowledge accrues, by a genuine affinity with the works of art. The blue-and-white Tang dynasty (1271–1368) *guan* (pot) which sold in 2005 to the London-based dealer Eskenazi for $27.7 million has been the last time to date that a significant Chinese work of art sold to a non-Chinese. The prices for Chinese ceramics mainly from the Ming (1368–1644) and Qing (1644–1911) dynasties have continued to rise ever since, culminating in the sale of a mid-seventeenth-century vase which achieved $82.3 million at Bainbridge, a small West London auction house, at the end of 2010 (although the bid was not thought to be honoured and the vase was eventually sold by Bonhams for about $38.75 million). Other areas of Chinese taste for their indigenous art have also come to the fore. In 2009 a regional English auction house, Wooley and Wallis, sold a rare and perfect jadeite buffalo, in the lunar year of the ox, to a Chinese buyer for $6.69 million. The significance of the auspiciousness of the object and the time at which it was purchased adds further reason to the impetus behind Chinese buying. In April 2010 in Hong Kong a white jade seal from the period of the Qianlong emperor (1711–99) made $12.4 million, double its 2007 price. Its value was enhanced by its close association with the emperor and the magical effects of a particular kind of nephrite (white jade) on Chinese sensibility.

Another element in the Chinese cultural jigsaw that has seen exponential growth is *guohua* or national art, a term forever associated with the anti- Manchu, pro-Chinese Republic artistic movement known as the *Lingnan* School. In November 2009 Poly, China's largest auction house, sold a scroll of eight Arhats by the Ming dynasty artist Wu Bin (1573–1620) to Liu Yiqian for $25 million. The final price exceeded the top estimate eight times. The market for *guohua*, and calligraphy in particular, was ignited in 2009. An example of the calligraphy of Huang Tinjian (1045–1105), *Pillar Ming*, fetched $66.8 million in the same year that Wu Bin achieved his record. There was a second crescendo in 2011 when an example of the modern artist Qi Baishi's (1864–1957) painting and calligraphy, *Eagle Standing in a Pine Tree with Four Character Couplet in Seal Script*, sold for a record $65 million in the spring sales at China Guardian auction house (see 'Art as Investment'). China's autumn sales usually outperform those held earlier in the year, and so the result was still more remarkable. Calligraphy commands a huge price today on the China market and is the biggest value driver, accounting for 60 per cent of the market in 2011.

Islamic art has seen a revival of interest from a wealthy Arab elite, which has in turn affected prices. In 2009 in Qatar, Sotheby's sold the nineteenth-century pearl carpet of Baroda to the ruling Al Thani family for $5.5 million. The next year, the sixteenth-century *kerman* carpet, a prototype design for the so-called *herati* pattern type showing two types of wool weft, sold at Christie's in London for $9.6 million. The seller, Georg Rehm, had acquired the rug for a relative pittance the year before. In spite of continuing political unrest in North Africa, the Levant and the Middle East, which has affected the mood of collectors, introduced a great deal of looted art onto the market and made it physically difficult to access and sell art from and in the region, another *kerman* carpet, the Clark Sickle Leaf, made a colossal $67.89 million at Sotheby's in 2013. A single leaf from the *Shahnameh* (book of kings) depicting Faridun in the guise of a dragon testing his sons, completed at the royal Safavid atelier (*c.*1525–35), sold at the same auction in London for $11.47 million.

Like China, there has been a keen interest amongst Arab collectors for their own historic cultural artefacts, in this case Islamic masterpieces. These objects are housed in new museum complexes primarily in the Gulf States. There has also been, characteristically of emerging markets at the beginning of their collecting cycle, a desire to buy modern oil paintings by indigenous masters and, in the case of the Arab market, European Orientalist oil painting. The same was certainly true in China in the 1990s and first decade of the millennium. The final push in the evolution of these markets from 'emerging' to 'developed' is usually signified by the acquisition of national contemporary art and blue-chip Western masterpieces for their public and large private collections. This has occurred spasmodically in China, although arguably the degree to which it is happening is overstated by the international art market. It has occurred partially in the Arab world. In those cases, the sole procurement agencies for both types of art are the ruling families of Qatar, the United Arab Emirates and the House of Saud.

The strict evolution of collectors' predilections does not always conform to the typical: traditional masterpieces, indigenous Modern, European Modern, national contemporary and blue-chip Western. Elsewhere, and in line with the traditional affection of emerging market collectors for local modernists, a painting of Balinese girls by the Mexican artist Miguel Covarrubias (1904–57), *Offering of Fruits for the Temple* (1932), made a record $1 million at Christie's, New York in 2011. Modernist predilections have also occurred in the Indian market, with record prices paid for artists of the Bombay Progressive Group (founded in 1947), and to a lesser extent in South East Asia, where there is a desire for the work of European émigrés such as Le Mayeur de Merpres (1880–1958), a member of the Mooi Indies

(Beautiful Indies) tradition. This emerging market preference for nostalgia and European realism afflicted the Taiwan market in the 1990s and is still present in China (see for example, the record sales of the Academic oil paintings of Xu Beihong (1895–1953)). When an emerging market matures, its taste moves towards tradition and nationalism. Marxist movements and states, observes Eric Hobsbawm, have tended to become national not only in form but in substance, and it could be argued this can be extended to include most territories who have autocratic governments. Post-colonial societies are reborn as nations and, very often, race-conscious ones, before the distant past is reclaimed. To this end, the Indian art market is showing signs of a shift away from the reformist, Western-centric progressive move-ment to the traditionally inspired work of artists from the Bengal School. Indian law still inhibits a trade in indigenous antiques, but the awareness of tradition is exemplified in the work of an artist like Nilima Sheikh (b.1945). Mindful of India's great residual craft tradition, Vibha Galhotra (b.1978) creates large sculptures made of ghungroos (ankle bells worn by Indian dancers) hand-stitched by local women. Another of her works, *Colony Collapse*, highlights the artist's gloomy prediction of the fate of the tene-brous emerging world's megacity (in her case Delhi). Indian international contemporary and modern art found favour in the West through alpha Indian dealers such as The Guild Gallery and Chemould, Prescott Road in Mumbai and Nature Morte in Delhi.

Pop art has had a broadly deleterious effect on the art of emerging markets because of its reflection of an individualistic, aspirational Western lifestyle largely at odds with the communalism and craft traditions of the great Oriental civilisations. It has spread like a contagion. This form of interna-tional contemporary art production has witnessed the most dramatic ascent in prices for Chinese artists who grew up during the Cultural Revolution (1966–71); artists who experienced the vanguard of a European ideology and culture – Marxism. Manga, a term used to describe the nineteenth-century 'sketches' of artists like Hokusai (1760–1849) and Hiroshige (1797–1858), grew into the comic-book characters that enjoyed a cult status in 1950s Japan. Manga had a limited success in its Chinese manifestation.

Another Pop art offshoot, active in Iran during this period and made material by Farhad Moshiri (b.1963), was sold at high prices at a series of international auctions in Dubai and Doha and the newly established Art Dubai fair. The art of Moshiri and that of the Iranian conceptual filmmaker and photographer Shirin Neshat (b.1957) depicts traditional tropes such as a water jar, Islamic calligraphy and the veil and hijab within a frivolous contemporary context.

The Brazilian artist Vik Muniz (b.1961) was equally afflicted by the aesthetics of Pop art and went on to enjoy major commercial success in New York (MoMa PS1). The South East Asian market, particularly Indonesia, produced a couple of Pop superstars, I Nyoman Masriadi (b.1973) and Agus Suwage (b.1959), whose work is modelled on that of the Northern Chinese realists. In Turkey, in spite of the country's notable list towards societal conservatism, the provocative super-realist Taner Ceylan (b.1967) produced his observations on Orientalism. Finally, orthodox Pakistan has given rise, if not rein, to the confrontational, and overtly sexual, photomontages of Rashid Rana (b.1968).

Most of this new art, with the exception of Indian contemporary and Modern painting, is supported by Western commercial interests; buyers, dealers and auction houses. Some is underpinned by Western curatorial expertise. Both Sotheby's and Christie's hold international auctions in China, Qatar, Dubai and, most recently, Mumbai. Alpha dealers like Lehmann Maupin, White Cube, Pace and Marlborough Fine Art represent a significant contingent of artists from emerging markets. In China, expatriate Western dealers like Boers Li and ShanghArt are still the most effective representatives of the cutting-edge. Most significant galleries in Europe and America hold emerging market stock.

The fact that a substantial body of this work 'floats' on the open market without institutional validation should be reason enough to fear for its future. Chinese speculators in Hong Kong 'flip' Political Pop works without first honouring their purchase bids. To flip a work of art is to sell it as quickly as possible after it has been bought. When a painting is confused with money to this extent a loss of confidence in its value is near at hand.

The new art from emerging markets, supported by an ideological shift as much as the economic and political rise of East Asia, China, India and South America, is forcing the international world of art and letters to address not fragmentation so much as polarisation. The transformation is best illustrated by the rise of an emerging market consensus that favours commonality and tradition (sometimes expressed as Archaism) over individualism and 'originality'. Most emerging market societies are choosing to re-examine and reinvigorate their past, which has led them to question the purpose of globalisation and the application to their civilisations of an international cultural standard. The assessment of this developing cultural accord will determine, ultimately, the fate of international contemporary art.

The art from emerging markets that is most likely to survive and bear scrutiny in the years to come, is work that reflects the culture from which it is drawn. It is therefore worth seeking out the new (abstract) calligraphers from Persia, the Middle East and China, or the work of communal crafts groups in India intent on reviving indigenous practices, revisiting the traditional skills of the Turkish jeweller or the Persianate and Anatolian carpet maker and artists who work in glass and stone. It is perhaps the local contemporary artists who work with these crafts and craftspeople who will be the ones who go on to produce enduring and valuable works of art.

Iain Robertson

Bibliography

en.artron.net

Blurton, T. Richard, *Hindu Art*, British Museum Press, 1992

Carmen Ramírez, Mari and Theresa Papanikoles, *Collecting Latin American Art for the 21st Century*, International Center for the Arts of the Americas, MFA Houston, 2002

De Bary, Theodore, *Sources of East Asian Tradition: Premodern Asia*, Columbia University Press, 2008, vol.1

De Las Casas, Bartolomé, *A Short Account of the Destruction of the Indies*, Penguin Classics, 2004

Faulkner, Rupert, *Japanese Studio Crafts: Tradition and the Avant-Garde*, Laurence King, 1995

Fernandes, Edna, *Holy Warriors: A Journey into the Heart of Indian Fundamentalism*, Portobello Books, 2007

Hobsbawm, Eric, 'Some Reflections on the "Break-up of Britain"', *New Left Review,* Sept–Oct 1977, vol.105

Hutton, Will, *The Writing on the Wall: China and the West in the 21st Century*, Abacus, 2007

Kerlogue, Fiona, *Arts of Southeast Asia,* Thames & Hudson, 2004

Mirza, Q. et al., *Rashid Rana: A World Apart*, Chatterjee & Lal Chemould, Prescott Road, 2010

Porter, Venetia, *Word into Art: Artists of the Modern Middle East*, British Museum Press, 2006

Robertson, Iain, *A New Art from Emerging Markets*, Lund Humphries, 2011

Robertson, Iain, *Understanding Art Markets: Inside the World of Art and Business*, Routledge, 2015

Takashi, Shiraishi, *Asian Modernism: Diverse Development in Indonesia, the Philippines and Thailand*, The Japan Foundation, 1995

OBJECTS

CONNOISSEURSHIP

Connoisseurship (from the French connaître: to know), being an expert in matters of taste, is particularly associated with the fine arts but is also connected to wine and food. It indicates an individual with a comprehensive knowledge and critical understanding of a subject. The theory is that repeated study of an art work will enable the viewer to get to know certain idiosyncratic traits particular to the artist and that ultimately this approach will assist in determining authorship and in distinguishing true from false – in other words to determine authenticity. In the twenty-first century, the role of the connoisseur is generally to establish who made the work, when and where. Since the 1960s the reputation of connoisseurship has declined in academe owing to the rise and pre-eminence of theoretical and sociological approaches to art history and to the decline in formalist approaches. In addition connoisseurship, with its implied interior and subjective understanding – particularly in relation to matters of taste – has been negatively associated with dilettantism. There has been a perception that connoisseurship lacked intellectual rigour and could not be taught as an academic subject. In addition, there continues to be the view linked to the history of connoisseurship that it is practised by a narrow elite. The connoisseur as a figure who passed judgement on quality in art and, also on occasion, on authenticity was valued increasingly in Europe from the eighteenth century. An examination of the history of connoisseurship over the last 200 years also reveals its prejudices, divisions and dichotomies. In the eighteenth century artist and collector Jonathan Richardson (1667–1745) held that connoisseurship made one a better gentleman. In 1816 the painter and writer Benjamin Robert Haydon (1786–1846) published an attack on the classical scholar and connoisseur Richard Payne Knight (1750–1824) after the latter had cast doubt on the authenticity of the Elgin Marbles. Haydon's attack focused on Payne Knight's position as a professionally untrained gentleman and connoisseur.

In the nineteenth century connoisseurship emerged as a major epistemological model for the study of art. A leading figure in the literature on connoisseurship was Giovanni Morelli (1816–91). Morelli is considered the inventor of scientific connoisseurship because of his emphasis on the close examination of anatomical detail. In *Italian Painters* (first published in 1890), Morelli articulated the view that each artist has their own idiosyncratic manner of creating (generally painting and drawing) which is most evident in areas such as the hand or ear or in the execution of drapery. In particular, he asserted that it was possible to see an artist's stylistic essence in the smallest physical details such as the fingernail, toenail or ear lobe. The art historian must operate like a detective since each artist leaves unconscious traces that are not necessarily followed by a pupil, thus enabling the connoisseur to distinguish the original from a copy. This approach was also thought to enable the expert to distinguish an original from a forgery. Morelli's method of discovering meaning in slight or unconscious detail was also of interest to Arthur Conan Doyle (1859–1930) and Sigmund Freud (1856–1939). Morelli stressed that the connoisseur focused on the work of art and regarded the art historian as a bookish pedant. For Morelli, the connoisseur engaged in long and careful study of the individual object in order to determine authorship and to ascertain quality. Morelli also appeared to associate connoisseurship with an elite who 'know' a great work of art when they see it. Morelli believed in two kinds of sight – physical and spiritual, with the spiritual expressed as belonging to artists and students of art who are both privileged and endowed with a natural gift and according to Morelli, after long and careful study are able to discern the deeper meanings in outward forms. This more subjective approach involving a spiritual and emotional response to art (most particularly paintings) has become increasingly discredited. That said, the Morellian method continues to be employed into the twenty-first century.

Morelli's connoisseurship was admired by a number of followers including Bernard Berenson (1865–1959), Adolfo Venturi (1856–1941) and Constance Jocelyn Ffoulkes (1858–1950). Bernard Berenson was the most influential and well-known disciple of the Morellian approach, which he articulated in his 1894 essay 'The Rudiments of Connoisseurship', published in 1902. An American by upbringing, Berenson emerged as the pre-eminent expert in Renaissance art in the late nineteenth century. His expertise proved particularly useful to collectors and dealers. He cultivated strong relationships with major US collectors such as Isabella Stewart Gardner (1840–1924). Berenson used his skill in attribution both to buy art and to advise his collectors. More controversially, he struck up a relationship with the art dealer Joseph Duveen (1869–1939) in 1906, later introducing Duveen to Mrs Gardner. Berenson continued to act as her adviser and apparently received a 25 per cent commission on resulting total sales from Duveen until 1928. From 1928 Berenson became less reliant on Duveen's commission from both purchases and sales and instead received a retainer. Duveen relied on Berenson's expert opinion to persuade collectors of the authenticity and quality of the works of art. Berenson's expertise thus had an enormous impact on the art market particularly with respect to prices for Old Masters and served to accelerate and enhance the market for this field since his assessment of an object's authenticity greatly increased its value. Berenson's numerous optimistic evaluations and his relationship with Duveen have led to doubt being cast on a number of his attributions. He appears to have conflated his role as a connoisseur with that of high social status, thus reminding us that today the status of connoisseurship may be compromised when this approach is used in the service of the market or for social advancement. It may not be coincidental that the decline in this aspect of connoisseurship's reputation dates from after Berenson's death.

Another significant development in the history of modern connoisseurship occurred as a result of a forgery case and associated lawsuit in 1945–7 when it emerged that a 'famous' painting by Johannes Vermeer (1632–75), thought to have been recently rediscovered, was in fact a forgery by Han van Meegeren (1889–1947). Van Meegeren was able to mislead a number of experts including connoisseurs and scientists, since he painted with pigments consistent with those used by the Old Masters. In addition, he painted on top of the surface of seventeenth-century paintings. His downfall was that he used a modern binding agent. One of the challenges for connoisseurship and a further reason that this approach fell into disrepute was that experts at the Van Meegeren trial had discussed the style of the painting in generic terms and made value judgements, referring to the work as demonstrating pure expression and a deep religious emotion. Such sentiments were difficult to prove and subject to widespread disagreement and debate.

The issue of the evaluation of expert knowledge is an ongoing one. The Van Meegeren case is significant as an instance of intuitive connoisseurship being downgraded, marking the beginning of a more 'scientific' approach to connoisseurship. The Rembrandt Research Project by the Netherlands Organisation for Scientific Research illustrates this transition. The project credited Morelli with having invented their techniques of connoisseurship – particularly in his focus on certain seemingly insignificant details. The approach of the project since the 1970s has also been to employ science to determine the authorship of works. The twenty-first-century connoisseur increasingly also needs to be familiar with scientific and technical processes including X-rays, infrared photography, Raman microscopy, pigment sampling, canvas research, multi-spectral imaging and dendrochronology. In addition, the expert needs to be able to analyse scientific data and use it in the service of connoisseurship. Scientific data may act as an aid to determine the age of the panel, canvas or pigment but it cannot be used to verify authorship. More recently the Rembrandt Research Project has confirmed that connoisseurship ultimately played a larger role in its conclusions than science, making the point that absolute certainty can seldom be proven in the making of attribution – particularly if unsupported by documentary evidence.

Connoisseurship is much debated in the twenty-first century, particularly in academe. As an approach it continues to be used by dealers, collectors and auctioneers, but there is a persistent view in the academic community that the status of connoisseurship continues to be low both in universities and in museums and galleries, although there has recently been a shift here owing to the rise in technical art history as a field of study in the US and Europe. Some commentators have asked whether there is a crisis of connoisseurship, noting that art history graduates seldom demonstrate connoisseurial skills. This view is largely owing to continuing negative associations of connoisseurship with both elitism and the art market and the prevailing perceived belief that connoisseurship, without a clear methodology, cannot be taught. More recently art professionals have asked whether object knowledge should be separated from technical elements of attribution and seemingly intuitive aesthetic judgement.

Connoisseurship may also be confused with visual acuity, which is more widely taught in universities. Here students are taught to be visually literate and to look closely at works of art to see what can be learnt from the object as part of a contextual analysis. This approach does not necessarily involve object handling or an engagement with questions of style, quality, authorship or date. Few, if any, university-level courses train students in connoisseurship and in the interpretation of scientific tests. There continues to be no methodology for attributions or handbooks to train aspiring connoisseurs – both necessary if the discipline is in fact more than a flash of intuition. That said, object-based art history continues to be taught at tertiary level in Europe and North America and the study of technical art history is increasing in universities. In the UK increasing numbers of universities are partnering with museums in joint PhD projects some of which engage in technical art-historical projects.

More recently, David Freedberg has written one of the strongest arguments outlining the reasons for connoisseurship continuing to matter and also being worthy of disciplinary esteem. Freedberg suggests that connoisseurship's interdisciplinary nature lies in its engagement with the sciences and social sciences. For example, the ability to determine quality and authorship of a group of drawings may involve working with experts in anatomy and natural history as well as archivists and paleographers. This both enlarges the field and also opens up the possibility of engaging with a much wider world. Connoisseurship occupies a role at the centre of the arts, humanities, sciences and social sciences – not just for the discipline of art history. This is because connoisseurship employs a myriad of different tools and also because it may offer an exemplary crossover between the new neurosciences and traditional historical ones, unpacking the science of how we apprehend, read and classify a work of art. In addition, Freedberg argues that rather than dismissing intuition, it is important to unpack the cognitive processes at work that include the role of intuition. Freedberg's analysis offers a multivalent and interesting way forward for connoisseurship and one that provides a conceptual, multidisciplinary and methodological underpinning to this approach.

Connoisseurship is more difficult to categorise with respect to contemporary art given that it has become increasingly context-based, with for example site-specific performance art. With respect to questions of authorship, this is less relevant for contemporary art since the artist is usually still alive and able to assist. Recent and contemporary artists may also actively resist connoisseurship and question associated issues such as quality, authorship and authenticity – Andy Warhol (1928–87) and Elaine Sturtevant (1924–2014) being cases in point. The rise of technical art history as a field of study in universities and the increasing number of PhD collaborations in Europe between museums and universities jointly committed to technical art history, together with David Freedberg's timely intervention, may signal a new direction for connoisseurship. (See also 'Authenticity').

Jos Hackforth-Jones

Bibliography

Barrett, Katy, 'The Educated Eye: Connoisseurship Now at the Paul Mellon Centre', *Apollo*, 6 May 2014

Berenson, Bernard, *Florentine Painters of the Renaissance,* G.P. Putnam's Sons, 1896

Berenson, Bernard, *Central Italian Painters of the Renaissance,* G.P. Putnam's Sons, 1897

Cumming, Robert (ed.), *My Dear BB; The Letters of Bernard Berenson and Kenneth Clark 1925–1959*, Yale University Press, 2015

Dictionary of Art Historians, https://dictionaryofarthistorians.org

Freedberg, David, 'Why Connoisseurship Matters', Columbia University Academic Commons, 2006, www.columbia.edu/cu/arthistory

Grosvenor, Bendor, blog, www.arthistorynews.com/categories/Conservation

Ginzburg, Carlo and Davin, Anna, 'Morelli, Freud and Sherlock Holmes: Clues and Scientific Method', *History Workshop*, Spring 1980, no.9

Morelli, Giovanni, *Italian Painters: Critical Studies of their Works,* trans. by C.J. Ffoulkes, John Murray, 1892

Sutton, Peter, 'Rembrandt and a Brief History of Connoisseurship', in Ronald Spencer (ed.), *The Expert versus the Object: Judging Fakes and False Attributions in the Visual Arts*, Oxford University Press, 2004

Tummers, Anna, *The Eye of the Connoisseur: Authenticating Paintings by Rembrandt and His Contemporaries*, Getty Publications, 2011

Uglow, Luke, 'Giovanni Morelli and his friend Giorgione: Connoisseurship, Science and Irony', *Journal of Art Historiography*, December 2014, no.11

AUTHENTICITY

The authentic refers to the real or genuine – particularly with respect to an author or painter. To authenticate means to give authority or legal validity to and to establish something as genuine or real, thus also certifying its origin or authorship. In relation to the visual arts, authenticity can be divided into two kinds of approach: physical or material authenticity and conceptual or contextual authenticity. Establishing physical/material authenticity involves an understanding of connoisseurship, provenance and technical art history together with an ability to read and interpret scientific data, plus a knowledge of appropriate scientific developments and approaches. Determining physical/material authenticity, then, is a complex and multidisciplinary process which also intersects with due diligence. (See 'Due Diligence'.)

In order to establish physical/material authenticity the expert begins by acquiring a thorough knowledge of the physical condition of the work of art via an empirical observation of its materials, techniques, condition and configuration in order to establish the date and to attribute authorship. This technical examination includes an analysis of any restoration carried out, since this has a bearing on both the quality of the work and its value. Some understanding of scientific process is vital in order to ascertain the degree to which a work may have been altered since its production. Typically an expert in a museum or commercial gallery will also need to research the work in order to find supporting documentary evidence which will attest to its provenance (the history of its ownership and location) and to the history of the work as well as to its authorship. Establishing physical/material authenticity is important both for the museum world and for the commercial sector. This process is integrally associated with three key modern institutions: the museum, the auction house and the art fair. Museums in particular perform a major role in validating authenticity and in promoting the acceptance of a work of art as authentic. Museums are thus equally the bastions and the gatekeepers of authenticity: in economic terms they play a vital role in securing the symbolic value of a work of art. This may increasingly lead to the enhancement of the economic value of that object.

As a starting point, dealers and gallerists are generally keen to identify the characteristics of a work and locate it in its particular cultural and artistic milieu as either an original work or a copy – be it in the school, circle or studio of a particular artist. (See also 'The Auction Process'.) Works of art are usually validated as either autographic, where they can be securely attributed to an artist, or prototypical, where they are determined to be typical and primary examples of the artist's oeuvre. Establishing material authenticity is particularly useful in relation to conventional media and to both modern and Old Masters.

In recent years there has been an increasing interest in technical art history in the Academy. In both Europe and the US there has been an acceleration in the technical and scientific research of art objects and an increasing number of courses of study in this field. The last decade has seen numerous exhibitions (mainly in the West) that invoke technical art history and the sciences alongside connoisseurship to address issues around authenticity in order to test attributions. The exhibition *Rembrandt: The Master and his Workshop* (1991) at the National Gallery, London, included recent re-attributions and the outcomes of the work of the Rembrandt Research Project. In 2010 the National Gallery's *Close Examination: Fakes, Mistakes and Discoveries*, with funding from the Engineering and Physical Sciences Research Council, was able to re-attribute a number of paintings where formerly attributions had been thought to be secure. The aim of this exhibition was to determine authenticity in as disinterested a manner as possible and to determine whether the exhibited works were indeed by the hand of the Master, or a workshop collaboration, period copy or a more recent forgery. This was a courageous exhibition in which connoisseurship and archival, technical and scientific expertise were jointly employed to re-attribute a painting to Raphael (1483–1520) formerly thought to be a copy and similarly to 'downgrade' a painting by Hans Holbein the Younger (c.1497–1543) to Michiel Coxcie (1499–1592). In considering authenticity in relation to Old Masters, it is important to remember that during and after the Renaissance, workshop practice meant that as part of their training artists would copy from their master. In addition to this practice, apprentices in a workshop would assist in the execution of a work and frequently made copies of the finished object as a record. Copies, then, were regularly made with no intention to deceive. (See 'Ethics'.)

Exhibitions that focus on artists' technique and involve scientific analysis alongside connoisseurship are becoming increasingly common on both sides of the Atlantic not only in relation to Old Masters but also in relation to twentieth-century art. In 2015 London's Estorick Collection's exhibition, *More than Meets the Eye: New Research on the Estorick Collection*, combined connoisseurship with science in order to enhance knowledge and understanding. In one case, the outcome meant that the gallery was able to refute the attribution of the artist himself, in this case *The Engineer's Mistress* (1929) by Carlo Carrà (1881–1966), where it emerged that Carrà had changed the date in order to please his patron's desire for an earlier and thus more valuable autographic work.

A number of exhibitions have also been devoted to the issue of fakes and forgeries. While an artist may make a fake in good faith, the production of a forgery implies deliberate deception in the making of a fraudulent imitation and is illegal. (See also 'Fakes, Forgeries and Thefts'.) There are numerous infamous cases over the last hundred years – most notably Han van Meegeren's forging of Vermeer's paintings that misled respected and high-profile experts. While it is becoming increasingly easier to detect later ground and materials, some more recent forgers have been able to successfully forge documentation and provenance – the so-called Bolton forger being a case in point. Shaun Greenhalgh made an alabaster forgery, *The Amarna Princess*, in the style of an Egyptian princess of 1350 BC. This was purchased in 2003 for $695,200 by Bolton Council who were convinced by the beauty of the work and by the added weight of forged documentation. The most infamous instance of document forging to support attributions is by John Drewe (b.1948). In the 1990s he was able to penetrate the archives of Tate, the Institute of Contemporary Arts and the Victoria and Albert Museum. He then changed the records of numerous artists so that they matched the forgeries painted by his associate John Myatt (b.1945). There continues to be uncertainty regarding the extent of Drewe's document forgery and tampering with archives. There is a great public appetite for the role of fakes and forgery in art crime. Exhibitions on this topic tend to attract large crowds, such as *The Metropolitan Police Service's Investigation of Fakes and Forgeries* exhibition held at the Victoria and Albert Museum in 2010, which had to be extended owing to the scale of public interest. The Art Loss Register, a comprehensive international database, continues to report that art forgery costs the UK art market alone at least $310 million a year.

Attempts to successfully authenticate art are ongoing and will continue – especially given the large sums at stake in the art market. One of the most compelling stories in recent years concerns the so-called *La Bella Principessa* – an unsigned drawing on vellum with no substantial provenance, which first came onto the market at a Christie's auction in 1998. It sold for $21,850, before being exhibited at Kate Ganz's gallery in 2007 where it was catalogued as nineteenth-century German School. It was purchased by Peter Silverman, who enlisted the support of numerous experts to employ technical and scientific analysis in order to endorse the work as an authentic drawing by Leonardo da Vinci (1452–1519). Much has been written about this drawing and expert opinions are divided – with the majority coming out against the attribution to Leonardo. Revealingly the drawing was not included in London's National Gallery exhibition of *Leonardo da Vinci: Painter at the Court of Milan* in 2011. It may be that the current owners' sensationalist marketing of this drawing and the fact that any judgement is perceived to lend weight to a process of sale has also deterred some experts from passing a judgement in its favour. The role of museums in the process of authentication is significant. Experts tend to avoid liability by confirming whether a work will or will not be included in a forthcoming exhibition or major catalogue. Conversely, *Christ as Salvator Mundi* (1490), also attributed to Leonardo da Vinci, was included in the National Gallery's exhibition in spite of some bad overpainting and some unconvincing sections in the work. There is, however, an etching of 1650 after this painting made by Wenceslaus Hollar (1607–77) which adds to the veracity of the attribution, and unlike *La Bella Principessa*, *Christ as Salvator Mundi* has an impressive provenance since it was once owned by Charles I and was recorded in his art collection prior to being auctioned in 1763. The painting was accepted by the National Gallery for its 2011–12 exhibition reportedly on the condition that it would not appear on the market for some time. It was sold to the Russian oligarch Dmitry Rybolovlev for \$127.5 million in 2013.

With respect to contemporary art, increasingly in academia there has been greater focus on the processes of replication so that art historians and their scientific counterparts consider casting techniques, stamping and striking images, printmaking techniques, photographic processes and replication. The issues of both physical and conceptual authenticity apply to contemporary art. With regard to physical authenticity, there is the added advantage of a living artist being able to assist in documenting the work. A number of museums such as the Guggenheim have focused on establishing new practices which will assist both in conserving contemporary art via the Variable Media Initiative (in particular performance and sound works and those of a more ephemeral nature) and in establishing and maintaining authenticity. When a work is acquired Guggenheim conservation staff contact the artist in order to confirm details about the material and production of the work of art, its exhibition history and any additional information regarding conditions of installation and the work's variability. In order to understand and preserve the art work, the museum considers that it is vital for the conservator to consider not only the artist's intention and the work's technical make-up but also the relationship between the two.

Conceptual or contextual authenticity is most consistently invoked in connection to contemporary art. In the late 1960s and 1970s many artists challenged definitions of authorship and originality. Art and Language, a conceptual artists' group founded in the late 1960s adopted a conceptual approach making works identical to the original. This practice would come to embody postmodernism and appropriationism in the 1980s. Conceptual or contextual authenticity occurs when an artist adopts a more conceptual approach and may separate the notion of authenticity from originality. Thus artists might appropriate, remake or reproduce the work of a (generally earlier) artist. The twenty-first-century remake may act in a subversive manner to undermine the authenticity of the original work and also to comment on the mistaken conflation between its price and value. Elaine Sturtevant is a case in point, deconstructing for the viewer the notion that a copy is necessarily a paler imitation, in her remakes of work by well-known artists such as Claes Oldenburg (b.1929), Andy Warhol or Jasper Johns (b.1930). Here Sturtevant reminds us that a work may be authentic but may not be an original.

Since the eighteenth century collectors have frequently tended to buy 'names'. In recent years a number of commentators have noted that mis-attributed works in museums, most notably those originally attributed to Rembrandt, have not only suffered in terms of the staggering drop in market value but also in the resulting decline in museum audiences for these works, following their reattribution. Cases in point are the Gemäldgalerie's *Man in a Golden Helmet* (*c.*1650) and the Frick Collection's *The Polish Rider* (*c.*1655). As well as the dramatic fall in both economic and symbolic value, neuro-aesthetics, the study of the effects of art objects on the brain, has established that parts of the brain, most particularly the orbitofrontal cortex, are more responsive to the 'art status' or authenticity of a work than to its sensory and aesthetic content, reminding us of what may be obvious to anyone who regularly visits museums, that knowledge of a work's authorship determines the reaction from the viewer.

Jos Hackforth-Jones

Bibliography

Aldrich, Megan and Jos Hackforth-Jones (eds), *Art and Authenticity*, Lund Humphries, 2012

Brown, Matthew, 'Traces of the Holy, the Contemporary Art Work as "Cryptorelic"', *Times Literary Supplement,* 14 October 2015

Freedberg, David, 'Why Connoisseurship Matters', Columbia University Academic Commons, 2006, www.columbia.edu/cu/arthistory

Hermens, Erma and Tina Fiske (eds), *Art Conservation and Authenticities*, Archetype Publications, 2009

Oxford English Dictionary

Salisbury, Laney and Aly Sujo, *Provenance: How a Con Man and a Forger Rewrote the History of Modern Art*, Penguin, 2010

Spencer, Ronald (ed.), *The Expert versus the Object: Judging Fakes and False Attributions in the Visual Arts*, Oxford University Press, 2004

Taylor, Paul, *Condition: The Aging of Art*, Paul Holberton Publishing, 2015

Tummers, Anna, *The Eye of the Connoisseur. Authenticating Paintings by Rembrandt and His Contemporaries*, Getty Publications, 2011

Weiseman, Marjorie. E., *A Closer Look: Deceptions & Discoveries*, National Gallery, 2010

FAKES, FORGERIES
AND THEFTS

Criminal activity in the art world, or art crime, is a subject that incorporates a range of illegal approaches to the ownership, integrity and identity of cultural objects. It is a multi-billion-pound black market that is extremely tempting for criminals through the accessibility of the objects involved, combined with the potentially very high rewards that come from works that break auction sale records. Theft by dispossession, theft by deception and theft by destruction collectively define our understanding of criminal activity in the art world, and these three phenomena provide the framework with which we will approach our analysis of this intriguing subject.

Theft by dispossession is manifest through the three distinct criminal offences of larceny, robbery and burglary. The motivation to engage in art theft ranges from ideological repatriation and protest against taxation, to money-laundering and financial advantage. However, the greatest challenge facing the art thief is the conversion or resale of the stolen object, as ownership records are widely available on the internet and the establishment of provenance is an important criterion to determine prior to the purchase of cultural objects. The following case studies aim to illustrate the challenges facing the art thief and the range of motivations behind their actions. On 21 August 1911, Vincenzo Perrugia, an employee in the Musée du Louvre, stole Leonardo da Vinci's *Mona Lisa* (1503–19) by concealing himself in a closet overnight and removing it from the museum concealed under a sheet. For Perrugia, stealing the painting was the first stage in what he viewed as a noble act of repatriation; his intention being to return the painting to its native Italy in the belief that it had been illegitimately acquired in the eighteenth century by Napoleon Bonaparte (1769–1821) as a war trophy. However, the ownership of the painting legally resided with the French state because it had been purchased by François I (1494–1597) upon the artist's death. Perrugia's act of political defiance illustrates one motivation for stealing the work; intriguingly, exactly 50 years later another act of political protest presaged the theft of a portrait of Napoleon's most famous military opponent. On 21 August 1961 John Bunton climbed over a back wall in London, slipped through an unlocked window of the National Gallery and stole the portrait of the Duke of Wellington (1812–14) by Francisco de Goya (1746–1828). Bunton's father, Kempton, used the media attention generated by the theft to highlight the financial difficulties faced by pensioners such as oppressive TV licensing fees. Four years later, the painting was recovered by the police and Kempton Bunton was charged under the Larceny Act of 1916. However, his conviction only amounted to the theft of a frame as they were unable to prove that he intended to permanently deprive the National Gallery of the painting. As a consequence of this episode, the Theft Act (1968) was enshrined in UK law, which eliminated the condition of 'intention to permanently deprive', and incorporated Section 11 which specifically applied to the 'removal of articles from places open to the public'. Although this event successfully captured the public imagination, not all art theft is ideologically motivated, as the audacious robbery of an important North American museum illustrates.

Early one morning on 18 March 1990, two thieves dressed as police officers gained entry into the Isabella Stewart Gardner Museum in Boston, Massachusetts. They handcuffed the two security guards on duty and stole 13 works of art, which included five works by Edgar Degas (1834–1917), three by Rembrandt (1606–69) and a single Vermeer (1632–75). Although the incentive for the theft was financial, its notoriety and those of the objects stolen made their potential resale on the open market virtually impossible. The current location of the works remains unknown and the museum continues to offer a $5 million reward for any information leading to their recovery. This incident reveals the challenges for criminals who attempt to convert stolen objects into currency, and highlights the ways in which art theft can be used as an instrument for organised crime. Art detective Charles Hill reinforces this appraisal of their motivation, especially as the stolen works have not resurfaced on the open market in over 25 years.

Four years later organised crime would again play a key role in thefts from a German museum and underscore the complexities facing those participating in their recovery. On 29 July 1994, two paintings by J.M.W. Turner (1775–1851) from the Tate Britain collection were stolen while on loan to an exhibition at the Schirn Kunsthalle in Frankfurt. After receiving a $35.52 million indemnification payment from the insurers, the gallery repurchased legal title to the works in 1998 for $13.04 million, with an additional $5.7 million in expenses apportioned to the recovery process. Although the specifics of these recovery payments attracted criticism for potentially establishing a benchmark for financing information, the paintings were successfully returned to the Tate by 2002. During their absence the paintings had functioned as collateral within the criminal market, with the potential to be traded for alternative illegal goods or services. This clandestine exchange value has been estimated by experts to be up to 10 per cent of open market value, and the recipients of the objects also have the option to return them to the legal owner in exchange for a potential ransom or recovery fee. These thefts were a manifestation of organised crime in which the criminals were motivated by financial gain, through the perceived black-market exchange value of the works and a potential ransom payment. Monies were distributed to facilitate their eventual repatriation to the Tate Gallery, which highlights the importance of preserving channels of communication throughout the negotiation process.

These four case studies highlight the various motivations for criminals engaging in art theft and the inherent difficulties of converting stolen property on the open market. And yet art thefts continue to occur and, although stolen art databases exist, a comprehensive public repository of information is yet to be established. It is vital that the market increases its self-enforcement as theft is often conducted with the aid of art market insiders, whose awareness of collections and market trends perpetuates this criminal activity.

Art forgery is the creation and selling of works of art which are falsely attributed to others. Forgers commonly target artists who use an abstract or simplified pictorial language, especially modernist painters, and often emulate the work of artists achieving high prices on the secondary art market. In contrast to the earlier examples, forgery is more distanced from organised crime, as although the motivation for the forger may be financial, it is more often a reaction to the critical reception of their artistic practice. Han van Meegeren, for example, created forgeries not only to demonstrate that his technical skill was aligned with that of eminent painters, but also to challenge the authority of leading critics and connoisseurs responsible for authenticating art. In fact, in 1950s Paris, the first investigator of this phenomenon was the policeman Guy Isnard, who established a specific unit designed to prosecute perpetrators of art forgery. Forgery persists as an evolving challenge to the art market in a number of ways. Firstly, denouncing an object as a forgery requires sufficient weight of argument against its authenticity. An idiosyncratic feature of this process, and indeed perhaps symbolic of the art market in general, is a lack of consensus regarding the various methodologies employed to determine the authenticity of cultural objects. Scientific and technical analysis, together with connoisseurship, are some of the most important tools employed by researchers to help identify forged works (see 'Connoisseurship and Authenticity'). On occasion, however, it appears that even the experts can be misled.

Han van Meegeren began his career as an art teacher but was unsuccessful in his ambition to establish himself as a professional artist. This dissatisfaction motivated him to undermine his critics and the art establishment by creating multiple forgeries, including those purporting to be by the artist Johannes Vermeer. By exploiting what he considered the credulity of art experts eager to discover an overlooked original, Van Meegeren used themes, motifs and techniques from the artist's catalogue to create a number of credible forgeries. Through the careful manipulation of paint and artist materials he was able to emulate the age and physicality of works by Vermeer, such as *The Supper at Emmaus* (1936–7), which at the time was considered an autograph original by contemporary experts. After the Second World War he was charged with high treason for selling *Woman Taken in Adultery* (1942), again purportedly by Vermeer, to Nazi Field Marshal Hermann Goering. The gravity of his trial required him to substantiate his authorship of the work within the courtroom setting, by painting *Jesus Among the Doctors* during proceedings to prove his deceit to the assembled experts. With hindsight these works appear to be fairly clumsy copies of the Delft master's art, but not all deception in the art world is exercised on canvas; it can also be applied to the memory or historical integrity of a work.

In *The Art of Forgery* (2015) Noah Charney identifies the phenomenon of the 'provenance trap', whereby the ownership and transaction history of an object is deliberately manipulated to legitimise it and affect its market performance. This forgery of the narrative is particularly pervasive in its subterfuge, as the deception targets not only the connoisseur but also the provenance researcher. Perhaps the most egregious example of this was committed between 1987 and 1994 by John Drewe. During this period, Drewe commissioned approximately 200 forgeries of important nineteenth- and twentieth-century artists from the painter John Myatt (b.1945), and systematically fabricated their official provenance records within the collections of various London art libraries and museums. By manipulating the records to incorporate the forgeries within official catalogues, he legitimated their perceived authenticity to subsequent provenance researchers.

More recently, in 2011, the prestigious Knoedler Gallery in New York became embroiled in a scandal involving the transaction of forgeries emulating artists such as Jackson Pollock (1912–56) and Mark Rothko (1903–70). The gallery sourced the works through third parties who assured their authenticity and provenance. The works were then sold for substantial sums to a number of important collectors. But in truth these paintings were produced over a number of years by Chinese painter Pei-Shan Quian (b.1940), and the gallery has subsequently closed as a result of ongoing legal proceedings. These works were considered forgeries so it is important to consider how they can be distinguished from fakes, as these terms are often used interchangeably or incorrectly applied. A forgery is an intentional imitation of an artist or style that is fraudulently represented to be authentic. The fabrication of a work with the intention to deceive classifies it as a forgery. In contrast, a fake is an original object that has been tampered with or modified from its original state to appear as the product of another artist. It is a genuine item that has been altered by someone at a later date to misrepresent its nature and origin. For example, the application of a false signature to an object with the intention to deceive a recipient over the nature of its authorship classifies it as a fake. For either of these processes to be prosecuted in court, a crime, usually fraud, must have been committed and the object must have entered the market. This contingency is important because the history of art is replete with examples of artists emulating their predecessors for practical training or inspiration. The recent reattribution of a purported portrait of Martin Luther is an interesting example of the incorporation of fake works into national public collections.

The *Portrait of Alexander Mornauer* (1460–88) was acquired in 1990 by the National Gallery in London as a depiction of Martin Luther by Hans Holbein the Younger (*c*.1497–1543). It was included in the 2010 exhibition *Close Examination: Fakes, Mistakes and Discoveries*, which revealed the process of scientific analysis through which it was identified as a fake and its authorship reattributed. Amongst other clues, the Prussian blue pigment used in the background to alter the curvature of the subject's hat was unavailable until the eighteenth century, well after Holbein had died, and may have been applied to increase the stylistic resemblance to other works by the famous artist. The application of this pigment may have been intended to deceive subsequent owners, which classifies it as a fake; in contrast, a forgery intends to deceive the viewer from the moment of its inception. The work has now been reattributed by the National Gallery to the Master of the Mornauer Portait. Circumstances such as this in which the authorship of a work is reattributed may have a negative impact upon its perceived market value. The authenticity of a work impacts upon its desirability for potential investors, which increases the potential for it to be considered as a store of value. Accordingly, deception within the art world is not confined to the brush of the atelier, but it also emerges in a more banal incarnation through the process of money-laundering.

The financialisation of art and the publicity given to high prices in the mainstream media has prompted investors to incorporate cultural objects within investment portfolios. This increases the potential for money-laundering as art is often considered a safer store of value than alternative assets or commodities. This risk is further compounded through the comparative portability of art objects, which enables them to be easily transported across the world. Discretion and anonymity are intrinsic components of the art trade and participants, such as dealers and auction houses, are obliged to conduct due diligence to identify the origins and legitimacy of transacted funds. For example, in the UK, Her Majesty's Revenue and Customs (HMRC) has established a $17,000 (or equivalent) cash purchasing threshold over which transactions may be monitored, in order to help identify and combat the transfer of illegitimate funds into the market. Although the same threshold applies across the European Union, it decreases to approximately $10,200 in the United States and increases to $104,300 in Switzerland. The art market remains a global network of personalities and transactions in which variants such as these coexist, which presents a challenge to participants seeking to establish a harmonised and effective approach to money-laundering regulation.

Theft by destruction is the most pervasive, most common and immediate form of criminal activity affecting the art world at present. It is the dissolution of the meaning and cultural significance of objects and their relationship to their surroundings through erosion or displacement. It is important to contextualise the narrative and sociopolitical implications of this cultural destruction, as individuals, nation states and ideological forces continue to decontextualise our shared cultural record. Historical examples include the transfer of artefacts by wealthy aristocrats participating in the Grand Tour, the military campaigns of expansionist European empires, the expropriation and dissolution of religious institutions, the eradication of linguistic and cultural traditions through the imposition of colonial value systems, and the continued looting and destruction of archaeological sites by actors such as so-called Islamic State (Daesh). As perhaps the greatest current threat to our collective cultural identity, it is necessary to first consider the impact of this ideological assault on the archaeological record of the Near East. Looting is the illegal excavation of objects by non-professionals from their original context with the intention of resale on the international market. This financial benefit incentivises people to participate in the process, although Daesh is also engaged in the ideologically motivated destruction of ancient archaeological monuments. To this end, in August 2015 the international media reported the capture of Palmyra in Syria and the destruction of its UNESCO World Heritage Site. This was a signal to the international community that Daesh's iconoclasm was intended to destroy the cultural legacy of the subjugated areas of Syria and Iraq. In effect, their actions may be interpreted as a physical and ideological assault on the myriad cultural histories that afford meaning and context to these unique locations within both countries.

Although this cultural destruction has achieved a broad social impact, more localised examples also have a meaningful impact on their surrounding communities. An example of this occurred in 2011 when the bronze sculpture *Two Forms (Divided Circle)* (1969) by Barbara Hepworth (1903–75) was stolen from Dulwich Park in South London, having resided in the public space for over 40 years and being insured for approximately $650,000. Its removal caused resentment and anger among the local population. The financial value of the physical material was enough of an incentive for thieves to disregard its cultural significance and remove it for resale as scrap metal. As a result, Conrad Shawcross (b.1975) was commissioned to create another work to fill the space, and *Three Perpetual Chords* was unveiled in 2015.

Criminal activity in the art world occurs through multiple channels and for a myriad of reasons. However, as we have seen, its impact is widespread and pernicious. Buoyed by reportage of a robust and somewhat beguiling international art market, its attraction to criminals is both unsurprising and an immediate cause for concern. Theft by dispossession, theft by deception and theft by destruction all contribute to the dilution of our social identity and undermine our collective cultural record.

Gareth Fletcher

Bibliography

Amore, Anthony M., *The Art of the Con: The Most Notorious Fakes, Frauds, and Forgeries in the Art World*, Palgrave Macmillan, 2015

Bazley, Tom, *Crimes of the Art World*, Praeger, 2010

Chappell, Duncan and Saskia Hufnagel (eds), *Contemporary Perspectives on the Detection, Investigation, and Prosecution of Art Crime: Australasian, European, and North American Perspectives*, Routledge, 2014

Charney, Noah, *The Art of Forgery: The Minds, Motives and Methods of Master Forgers*, Phaidon, 2015

Charney, Noah (ed.), *Art Crime: Terrorists, Tomb Raiders, Forgers and Thieves*, Palgrave, 2016

Conklin, John E., *Art Crime*, Praeger, 1994

Keats, Jonathon, *Forged: Why Fakes Are the Great Art of Our Age*, Oxford University Press, 2013

www.legislation.gov.uk, *Theft Act 1968*

Lindsay, Ivan, *The History of Loot and Stolen Art: From Antiquity Until the Present Day*, Unicorn Press, 2013

Nairne, Sandy, *Art Theft and the Case of the Stolen Turners*, Reaktion Books, 2012

Radnóti, Sádnor, *The Fake: Forgery and Its Place in Art*, Rowman & Littlefield Publishers, 1999

Watson, Peter, *The Medici Conspiracy: The Illicit Journey of Looted Antiquities – From Italy's Tomb Raiders to the World's Greatest Museums*, Public Affairs, 2007

CONSERVATION
AND THE MARKET

Preservation, conservation, and restoration all play crucial roles in terms of how a work of art is maintained today, and ultimately how it will be viewed and valued in the future. For the owner and custodian of a work of art, there are several measures one can implement to ensure its safekeeping. Keeping a work of art in good condition relies upon a stable environment, appropriate handling, storage and display, and being able to assess when restorative measures are necessary. A trained, professional conservator can provide guidance and undertake treatments to slow deterioration, stabilise conditions and repair a work of art.

The term conservation has often been used in the art market as an umbrella concept to capture efforts to prevent, impede or repair the loss or deterioration of works of art. The contemporary viewpoint sees conservation and restoration as part of the same professional activity. As such, this discipline encompasses varied treatments that can be defined as preventative conservation, remedial conservation and restoration. Within the broadest context of contemporary practice, the term conservation has moved beyond preventative and interventive conservation practices to include information preservation, collections management, conservation science and research. Today the field has been broadened to deal with the challenges raised by modern and contemporary art practices. Advances in traditional materials, new media and technology within fine art require innovative treatment and technical study. The following will define the parameters of conservation practices, before exploring their relationship to contemporary art and the market.

Preventative conservation refers to any actions taken to stabilise the environment and minimise future loss of a work of art. While it is axiomatic that works of art, like all things, will age and deteriorate over time, preventative conservation is intended to slow deterioration; its objective is to mitigate the effects of deteriorative agents such as heat, light and moisture. Preventative conservation can include storage and display techniques that control the environment. These include climate conditions (control of relative humidity, temperature, light and atmospheric pollutants) and the use of acid-free storage materials that do not degrade or react with the art work. Proper framing, storage and handling of works of art will all help to prevent mechanical and chemical deterioration of materials. Creating safe conditions reduces the need for future invasive conservation or restoration campaigns. Beyond this, preventative conservation can be viewed as part of collection management, including the appropriate documentation and archiving of relevant data on the work of art.

Remedial conservation is best understood as the maintenance of a work of art, and can include any act impeding current damage or stabilising the structure of the object. In practice, conservators carry out practical interventions that are both aesthetic and preventative. For example, if the original linen of a canvas is degraded, relining the painting with new fabric may be necessary to enable it to be placed onto a stretcher for display, while also protecting the original canvas from environmental fluctuations, thus preventing future deterioration. Beyond remedial conservation, restoration is aimed at facilitating our ability to read a work of art. While these interventions may alter the current appearance of the object, the objective is to bring the object closer to its documented past condition. Examples of restoration may include reassembling a broken object. In another example, from 2012 to 2014 Tate restored the painting *Black on Maroon* by Mark Rothko, following an incident when a visitor to the museum graffitied the work of art with black spray-paint. Tate conservator Rachel Barker restored the work, carefully researching before cleaning and retouching the surface, thus returning the painting to a displayable condition.

Returning an object to an original or perfect state has long been abandoned in conservation as a Sisyphean ideal. Indeed, 'original' is a problematic term. It is never possible to reproduce exactly the original materials or condition, nor is that necessarily desirable in all art market sectors. For example, it is becoming increasingly commonplace in the market for contemporary art to replace defunct components such as a burned-out bulb in a fluorescent light work by Dan Flavin (1933–96). These measures allow these works of art to function, albeit at the expense of original components. Instead of endeavouring to return an object to an original state, contemporary approaches to conservation typically aim to facilitate reading of the artefact and simultaneously stabilise the material integrity of the object.

To answer what is the current best practice in conservation, it is useful to look at the work carried out in leading museums together with codes of practice published by international professional organisations. However, codes of practice that inform museum decisions about conservation and display may not always be followed in the treatment of privately owned works of art. Principles of reversibility and minimal intervention are important considerations for conservation decision-making. These principles have been reassessed in recent years, and it has been largely agreed within the conservation profession that achieving complete reversibility is often unachievable in practice. While historically the concept of reversibility (the application of restoration or conservation techniques which may be fully reversed) has been held up within museums as best practice, there has been a collective shift toward retreatable or sustainable treatments that can be safely removed in future. For example, although cleaning is irreversible, it ensures the safety of the object today, and provides future conservators with choices as to how they treat the object in future.

Within museums, best practice for preventative conservation begins with the assessment of works of art at the acquisition stage and continues through the implementation of policies on environmental conditions and the handling and storage of objects. This provides an ideal model for private collectors but ultimately the decision to maintain an art work is at their discretion. Not unlike museum practice, private conservators must also consider the demands on the works they conserve, and assess the condition of the work of art and its environment, as well as appreciate the requirements of the client. For private collectors, assessing the condition of an object at the point of acquisition mitigates the deterioration of works of art, and indirectly ensures that the object will not depreciate due to damage. Private conservators will endeavour to incorporate best practice as much as possible, but the market's expectations of conservation can often differ from best-practice standards developed by museums. While private conservators can advise on treatment informed by conservation ethics, a private collector's demand on the work may differ from that of museum collection. Guided by the input of multiple stakeholders and experts within the market, adaptive ethics refers to the negotiation that takes place among key decision makers.

Each treatment should start with an examination of the object to assess its materiality, condition, stability and the cause of its deterioration. This technical examination should be fully documented and archived. Such methodology encourages an interdisciplinary approach that invites collaboration with artists, scientists and art world and market professionals. At the heart of this exploration is the need to identify the function of the artefact in terms of the artist's practice and the owner's collection. The status of the work can also be understood in terms of its use or function as a documentary object providing insight into its cultural significance. Once conservators have considered these factors, the goals for treatment are determined based on technical and material constraints. It is critical to research both a work of art's context and its physical and material history. This involves delving into the history of an artist's working process and providing insight into their practices, materials and methods. For example, removing surface dirt from an unvarnished painting with water requires consideration to ensure that the paint is not water-soluble. The use of unorthodox mixed media in contemporary art, such as the use of fat by Joseph Beuys (1921–86), requires an understanding both of the materials and of their application by artists. Let us not forget, there is not always a logical reason why an artist has selected certain materials or made a work in a certain way, but understanding how a work of art is constructed may inform approaches to conservation.

Contemporary art offers an opportunity to seek the perspective and ratification of living artists in the conservation of their works of art. Working with an artist offers invaluable first-hand information about their methods and original materials, which may be vital information to document if materiality is considered to be of importance. But inviting artists to revisit a work of art can be unpredictable, and may introduce further challenges for conservation. While a conservator may strive for minimum intervention, an artist might initiate a more complex intervention, such as significantly reworking or retouching. Artists can and do change their minds. It may be the case that an artist's contribution will result in a larger intervention than a conservator would undertake independently.

The sheer variety of processes employed by artists today requires conservation expertise in identifying a multitude of techniques. With the rapid development of new artistic materials such as acrylic paint and adhesive tapes in the twentieth century, there has been a consistent trend amongst contemporary artists to experiment and exploit their properties to new ends. The post-war period represents a key moment of change not only in international contemporary art but also in the development and expansion of the field of conservation. The role of the contemporary art conservator has had to adapt in order to accommodate the variety of new media. The obsolescence of technology and the complications involved in documenting and installing time-based media have resulted in increasingly inventive and technical conservation strategies, ranging from replacing elements and creating multiples, to replicating entire works. Museums have adopted strategies for acquiring digital hard drives for new media works and stockpiling materials to facilitate the systematic replacement of short-lived elements in the future. For example, the conservation of *Untitled (Piano)* by Nam June Paik (1932–2006) at the Museum of Modern Art, New York, included replacing the cathode ray tubes in the original monitor to allow for its continued use, while upgrading the obsolete floppy-disc player with a wireless MP3 player.

In the tradition of twentieth-century art movements, a parallel development can be traced of artists who share interests in process and materiality (and indeed immateriality), and above all, call into question the autonomy and relevance of the art object itself. Such practices have changed the physical nature of the art object, and have introduced new material concerns. For instance, how does one conserve a Dieter Roth (1930–88) sculpture made of chocolate, sugar or mould? Conservators must strike a balance between respecting the intended impermanence of the work of art and managing the inherent volatility of materials. While the intention of preventative conservation aims at retarding deterioration or decay, the field has developed to accommodate ephemeral works of art and the need to mediate material change. In cases of this kind, the conservator and other invested decision makers will need to interpret what is authentic for the work of art. While condition has a significant influence on the price of conventional works of art such as oil paintings or prints, the prospect of duration is arguably no longer an indicator of value for some examples of ephemeral contemporary art. This is especially the case for works in which the aesthetic of decay is meant to convey meaning. This can be demonstrated acutely in the practice of Gustav Metzger (b.1926) or Anya Gallaccio (b.1923), where the experience of an ephemeral work of art is based in part on witnessing its decay and acknowledging its relatively short lifespan. While embracing innovative new conservation techniques, the ethical principles and scientific concepts underpinning the practice do not change when approaching even the most volatile of contemporary art works.

The question remains, how does the market view conservation? Condition issues and conservation have a significant impact on both the aesthetic and economic value of pieces in the art market. Generally insurance and auction appraisals will assess the condition of a work of art, including any damage and restoration, in its valuation since these factors have a direct impact on the valuation of a work. For instance, condition is an essential pricing factor for the prints market, and a print with fresh colour will generally garner a high estimate compared to duller versions. Significantly, once a print has faded, it is not possible to restore the work to its former vibrancy. The same is true of many other media. In this way, generally speaking, the state of preservation and condition will influence the value of a work. In theory its value should not diminish due to conservation or restoration. Indeed, if anything the value should be enhanced by such interventions.

It is important to note that the condition of an object may be weighted differently across market sectors. Expectations, expertise and taste about conservation will vary across market sectors. While it might at first appear that the extent of restoration is significantly more substantial for Old Master works of art compared to contemporary art, this is not always the case. Collectors often find a small blemish on the smooth surface of household gloss paint to be more visible or distracting than on impasto oil paint. Contemporary paints such as acrylics may take up to thirty years to fully dry, making these surfaces delicate and subject to damage. In the market for contemporary art the aesthetic of the 'new' epitomised in minimalist sculptures or ultra-glossy photographs demands pristine surfaces. Contemporary works of art such as stainless-steel sculptures by Jeff Koons (b.1955) require careful handling to protect their mirror-polished and transparent colour coatings. For these reasons, from the outset preventative conservation is crucial for maintaining the condition and value of these works.

The taste of decision makers in the private market can often dictate the extent to which a work of art is to be restored. In the Old Master sector, changes in attitude and practice mean that past campaigns may now be seen as aggressive. A painting may have been subjected to numerous conservation campaigns over the years. It is often the case in the Old Master market that restoration is undertaken to undo the damage of previous conservation or restoration treatments, such as removing significant over-painting. As we cannot ask the intention of the Old Master artists, research is required to understand the context and possible meaning of works of art in order to fill in the gaps, metaphorically or literally. Restoration decisions must be undertaken ethically, respecting the history of the object and the integrity of existing original materials. Present-day conservation practice advocates lining canvases to add structural integrity, but many market players still regard this practice with some scepticism. Taste also varies across market sectors. For example, the fragile nature of porcelain means that objects will often suffer damage, and collectors may be more accepting of cracks and repairs than in other sectors. In the Chinese ceramics market, while firing flaws or kiln dust may be considered acceptable for non-Imperial-quality porcelain, the market demands mint-condition Imperial marked ceramics, as the craftsmanship and artistry was generally of a higher standard. In these instances, it is the objects in the best condition with the least conservation or restoration that will garner the highest prices.

Select private collectors in the antiquities or Chinese ceramics market will favour invisible restoration for this reason. Troublingly, invisible repair is often achieved by spraying varnishes extensively over the original surface. Not only do these treatments mislead the eye, but they are also notoriously difficult to remove. Fortunately, there are various tools and technologies to detect damage and invisible repairs. For example, conservation studios are equipped with X-ray and infrared equipment to detect under-paint. For the private collector, a hand-held ultraviolet light is a useful tool to highlight areas that have been overpainted, touched up or previously damaged.

In the ceramics market, various 'tricks of the trade' for identifying restoration can be observed. These include idiosyncratic practices such as dragging a coin along a dish to detect a stutter, or listening for a clear, resonant ring when the edge of a plate is tapped. While a trained connoisseur may detect genuine porcelain by the sheen of a glaze or the weight of an object, it should be noted that even a cracked or broken piece of china might still ring. For this reason, it is advisable for collectors to refer to professional condition reports before buying. These documents, provided at auction and commercial galleries upon request, can also be acquired from trained conservators. Professional condition reports may save collectors significant amounts of money, and enable prospective buyers to understand the actual condition of a work of art. It can be costly to maintain collections in conditions that minimise the risk of deterioration of materials. Thus, these reports and preventative conservation and/or restoration should be considered as part of the incidental expenses beyond the initial cost of a work of art, just as the buyer's commission, taxes, duties, shipping, framing, installation and insurance are all necessary considerations. The allocation of resources to the conservation/restoration process should be factored into the full cost estimate of a work of art and regarded as an important stage in investing in an art collection.

Both condition and value are reassessed when works are prepared for loan, display or sale. For this reason, conservation and restoration work often precedes a work of art being sold at auction or through commercial galleries. In contrast to museums, private conservation studios will often receive works of art that are in the process of being bought or sold. Collectors are not obligated to work with a professional conservator. Dealers and auction house specialists will often suggest to consigners that a work be treated, and regularly cooperate with private conservation studios to oversee this work. To this end, it has become the custom of many large commercial galleries to have conservators on staff to check condition and stabilise works of art as they enter and exit galleries, and also provide advice to clients. While conservation decisions may be financially motivated for the owner of the work of art, in many cases a conservation treatment may not align with the values of the client. For example, high-gloss, chromogenic print photographs are incredibly light-sensitive, and exposure to light will result in fading or disappearing images. The ideal storage of a photograph may require total darkness; however, this option will not satisfy an owner's desire to appreciate the purchase.

Ultimately, preservation, conservation and restoration are value-led judgements based on technical and contextual information. With multiple decision makers having an emotional and financial stake in works of art, treatments should reflect not only stakeholders' values but also basic conservation principles that advocate that all works are treated with the same high degree of care regardless of the economic interests. A balance must be struck, therefore, between the ethical principles and what is in the best interest of the work of art and its stakeholders. It has been demonstrated that conservation decisions have a direct impact on the appearance and value of works of art. The measures adopted by the present generation of decision makers will dictate how the works look and are to be valued in the future. We are mere custodians of works of art while they are in our possession.

Yasmin Railton

Bibliography

Allington-Jones, Lu, 'The Phoenix: The Role of Conservation Ethics in the Development of St Pancras Railway Station (London, UK)', *Journal of Conservation and Museum Studies*, 2013, vol.11, no.1, Art. 1.

Buskirk, Martha, *The Contingent Object of Contemporary Art*, Cambridge, MIT Press, 2003

Caple, Chris, *Conservation Skills: Judgement, Method and Decision Making*, Routledge, 2000

Chiantore, Oscar, and Antonio Rava, *Conserving Contemporary Art: Issues, Methods, Materials, and Research*, Getty Conservation Institute, Los Angeles, 2012

Child, Robert, 'Ethics and Conservation' in Gary Edson (ed.), *Museum Ethics*, Routledge, 1997, pp 207–15

Coddington, James, Carol Mancusi-Ungaro and Kirk Varnedoe, 'Time and Change: A Discussion about the Conservation of Modern and Contemporary Art', *Conservation: The Getty Conservation Institute Newsletter*, Fall 2002, no.17, pp 11–17

Corzo, Miguel Angel (ed.), *Mortality Immortality?: The Legacy of 20th-Century Art*, Getty Conservation Institute, 1999

ICOM-CC, *Terminology to Characterize the Conservation of Tangible Cultural Heritage*, 15th Triennial Conference, New Delhi, 22–26 September 2008, www.icom-cc.org/.../icom-cc-resolution-terminology-english/

Muñoz Viñas, Salvador, *Contemporary Theory of Conservation*, Routledge, 2011

Van Saaze, Vivian, *Installation Art and the Museum*, Amsterdam University Press, 2013

ART AND LAW

RIGHTS OF ARTISTS

There is a common sentiment, particularly in the West, that *art is different* and that there should be certain fundamental rights enjoyed by artists that are of a different nature from, or go beyond, the rights of ordinary people as regards any art produced and the process for its production. However, the nature and extent of any such rights provoke considerable debate. There are few universally recognised rights for artists and, where such rights are contemplated, their implementation falls short of universal. The treatment of art and artists remains dependent upon the history, culture, politics and sometimes religion of the regions in which the artist lives, works, exhibits or sells. The issue of artists' rights goes to the core of how a society and a culture views art itself, and in so doing reflects upon the history and mores of each society touched by the art and the artist concerned.

A consequence of this diversity is that artists from different cultures find that they have radically different roles and rights from place to place, both in relation to their status and work as a whole and also in relation to the individual works of art they create. Countries in the Western world have attempted for more than a century to harmonise and codify a range of artists' rights, in a desire to provide a more unified system for the identification and of such rights, wherever the artist should operate or be appreciated. Much of the system thus created has more recently been adopted in the East. However, while these unification efforts have met with partial success in East and West, they nevertheless remain subject to the customs, culture and interpretation of individual countries. This means that even where states have signed up to a particular set of rules, such as, for example, those contained in the international conventions on copyright, these rules still have to allow for domestic variation and interpretation.

The right of freedom of expression is deemed to be a fundamental right in many countries and to be the basis for democratic government, but is not of course universally accepted around the world or even consistently applied by the most prominent democracies. Freedom of expression nevertheless provides a reasonable base upon which the rights of artists must rest, as restriction of the freedom to express oneself must necessarily impinge upon the creation of art and the rights of the artist to comment, question and challenge. Along with other rights seen as fundamental to a free society, freedom of expression is countered by a duty not to harm similar rights held by others, and each country's balance between these rights and duties is reflected in its attitude to art and to artists. This touches on the relationship between the artist as citizen and the state (or states) in which they are active, and extends to the relationships between artists and the owners of their art and also to relationships between artists and other artists.

The most common restrictions on artists' freedom of expression occur in states and societies where religious and/or political customs and laws provide, from the outset and at their core, for boundaries on political, religious or social comment. However, even in countries such as the US or UK which expressly defend freedom of expression (whether constitutionally or by custom), restrictions on artists' freedom of expression still occur, for instance around the perception that a particular expression offends public decency or dignity, as interpreted by the courts from time to time (and in the US, from state to state). Challenges to over artists' freedom of expression have accordingly arisen in conflicts between artists and those tasked with enforcing the obscenity laws in the artist's country. Famous examples in the UK have been the *Lady Chatterley's Lover* (1928) and *Oz* magazine trials, which effectively reduced restrictions on freedom of expression under the 1959 Obscene Publications Act, in 1960/61 and 1970/71 respectively. Similar issues have arisen in the US, examining the relationship between the prevention of public obscenity on the one hand, and the rights of free speech enshrined in the First Amendment on the other. While more recent obscenity cases in the US have tended to focus on the line between obscene pornography and the right of free speech, new challenges concerning works of art *per se* appear to have focused on the use of public funds for the exhibition of works that some might consider obscene, rather than directly on the rights of the artist to produce the work itself, as with Brooklyn Institute of Art and Sciences v City of New York and Rudolph W. Giuliani in 1999.

The legal rights of artists to control and protect their own artistic creations historically derived from two ideological roots, one primarily cultural and the other primarily commercial, and these roots continue to influence the application and extent of artists' rights even in today's increasingly globalised art world. The approach to artists' rights with its roots in France has been developed from a recognition of the 'otherness' of an original work of art and the creative process behind it, with a tangible link to the personality and creativity of the artist. The rights thus derived (sometimes collectively described as *droits d'auteur*) are deemed to be personal to the artist and derived from a form of natural right, being something more than a legal right that could otherwise be waived, assigned or circumscribed. On the other hand, artists' rights developed in common law countries such as the UK and US have a more commercial and less individual basis; legal protections for artists in this environment have been based principally on the protection of the artist's commercial interests (recognising however that an artist's reputation and integrity might have commercial attributes). In this legal framework, works of art are treated as assets which are created, bought and sold with much the same freedoms and restrictions as other assets. In the UK, ownership of a mass-produced piece of furniture historically gave rise to similar rights, restrictions and obligations as ownership of a painting. In France, to the contrary, the originality of the painting and the creative process behind it, aligned with the individual personality of the artist, would give rise to a more extensive set of rights for the artist, and the law would recognise a qualitative distinction between ownership of a mere asset and ownership of an original work of art.

These different approaches are seen today in the related areas of copyright and 'moral rights'. In both areas the last hundred years or so have seen efforts to harmonise different national laws, with the goal of providing artists with identical or comparable rights wherever they work, exhibit and sell their art. The difference, however, in conception and approach between the two systems described above continues to affect both the extent of harmonisation in the laws themselves, and the national application in practice of these supposedly harmonised laws. The first right specific to artists (and other creatives) to be the subject of international attempts at harmonisation was copyright; broadly the right to protect an original work from being copied without the creator's consent (and ability to charge). Versions of this right have long been upheld in various countries, and in the UK for instance can be traced back to the reign of Queen Anne (1665–1714). Copyright remains at base a national rather than an international or universal legal right. Since the Berne Convention of 1886 it has been given the appearance of universality through signatory countries' attempts to provide equivalent or matching copyright protections to the works of nationals of other signatory countries. Broadly, the Berne Convention ensured that each signatory country should protect the works of artists of other signatories to the same extent as it protected the works of its own artists. Here too, the two distinct roots for artists' rights are clearly discernible: the French-inspired *droits d'auteur* distinct from the perhaps more prosaic protection of economic rights underpinning the common law systems for copyright in the UK and US. The basic requirements of a national copyright law have been to a large degree harmonised by the Berne Convention and its successors; an original work should be protected from unauthorised copying during the life of its creator and for a fixed period thereafter (in most cases 70 years), and during such period the creator and their heirs should both control the making of copies of their work and enjoy the benefits deriving therefrom.

Several regional and national differences remain, however, many of which can be traced back to the divergent cultural roots for artists' rights. The first issue arises with identification of items capable of copyright protection. In France, the emphasis on the originality and creativity in the work and the artistic process behind its production, with its close relation to the individuality and personality of the artist, means that the level of required originality for a work to benefit from copyright protection is relatively high in comparison with the UK. The UK, on the other hand, has tended to place more emphasis on whether the degree of work and skill expended in the creation of the object justifies the protection of the economic benefits deriving from reproduction of the object (with less importance being attributed to the creativity or artistic merit of the work *per se*). This can lead to works (for example photographs) having a different status around the world and benefiting or not benefiting from copyright protection, depending on each national court's need to apply its own rules to assess whether the photograph was an original creation in its own right (achieving copyright protection), or simply the result of a mechanical process to reproduce its subject (which generally would fall short for copyright protection).

There can still be traps for the unwary, even where national legal systems have similar legal and cultural roots (and a common language). It is common ground that certain uses of copyright material should not be treated as infringing the artist's copyright. In the UK some of these exceptions to copyright protection are grouped under the heading 'fair dealing'; in the US the equivalent term is 'fair use'. Unfortunately these similar terms conceal different approaches, and it is not the case that a copy allowed in the US under the doctrine of fair use would necessarily be allowed in the UK under the doctrine of fair dealing. These discrepancies are becoming more of a problem in our increasingly digitised and globalised world; a 'thumb-nail' image of a copyright work uploaded to the internet in the US would generally be accepted there as not infringing fair use, but would not (absent qualification under a different provision) have an equivalent protection under the narrower doctrine of fair dealing if downloaded for viewing in the UK.

Copyright protections are concerned with the making and use of repro-ductions of an original work of art, with an emphasis on the protection of economic rights around use of such reproductions. In France, however, the special treatment of art and the creative process gave rise to a separate suite of rights for artists known collectively as the *droit morale* or moral rights, which sit alongside copyright. The most important of these concern the rights of Paternity or Authorship (to have one's creations correctly attributed), Integrity (the right to prevent unauthorised alteration of a work), Disclosure (the right to decide when a work is fit for first exhibition or distribution) and Modification (the right to withdraw, amend and update written works, subject to compensation for publishers' costs). These rights give artists in France a considerable degree of control over their works of art, even after the works have been sold, as they derive from the personality and creativity of the individual artist and are not related to, or limited by, laws of contract, ownership or possession of the work of art itself. This was perhaps a hard lesson for Sir William Eden (1849–1915), who, having commissioned James McNeill Whistler (1834–1903) to paint a portrait of Lady Eden in Paris in 1892, discovered that he was unable to compel delivery of the finished work when Whistler decided not to release it, even though he had paid for it. Presumably Sir William had considered that delivery of the painting would be subject to the terms of the commissioning contract (as would have been the case in the UK) but in France any such contractual terms could not override Whistler's right to refuse disclosure or distribution of the work on the grounds that he was not happy with it.

In contrast to countries deriving their approach from the French model, the law in the UK did not recognise a separate category of moral rights until 1989, under the 1988 Copyright, Designs and Patents Act. The US similarly introduced federal laws protecting moral rights under the 1990 Visual Artists Rights Act. In both cases the introduction of such new concepts was in response to the requirements of the Berne Convention that signatory countries should recognise certain moral rights within, and so far as permitted by, the parameters of their own legislation. In so providing, the Convention recognised and enshrined a degree of cultural and legal diversity in the scope and implementation of supposedly harmonised rights. The US and UK moral rights differ from each other in certain respects, but are both of substantially more restricted scope than the equivalent rights in France, even after harmonisation through Berne. The UK, for example, introduced moral rights of Paternity and Integrity, but provided that these rights should be capable of waiver by artists, and restricted the right of Paternity to cases where it had been previously 'asserted' by the artist in relevant contracts and notices. In France, such rights exist automatically, without condition and cannot be waived (and the list of enforceable moral rights is longer). Moral rights have been enacted in various forms around the world. In 1990 China introduced an extended set of authors' rights (updated in 2000) under the general copyright banner, and included rights of Publication, Authorship, Alteration and Integrity analogous to European moral rights and which (excepting Publication) are perpetual, whereas other Chinese copyright protections only last for the life of the author plus 50 years. In 2000, Australia similarly added moral rights of Attribution, Non False Attribution and Integrity to its existing copyright legislation. It remains the case that the extent and duration of the moral rights granted by individual countries varies at many levels from country to country.

Even where similar moral rights for artists have been enacted, their interpretation and practical enforcement is dependent upon location, as with copyright, reflecting the different cultural roots of the countries concerned. In the UK, when addressing the question of whether an artist's work has suffered derogatory treatment so as to prejudice the artist's reputation, the courts have applied an evidential and objective basis for assessment; effectively, can the artist produce clear evidence that a reasonable person (other than the artist) would consider the treatment to be derogatory and prejudicial? In France on the other hand, the courts would focus much more strongly on the subjective view of the artist. If the artist feels that their work has suffered derogatory treatment, which is prejudicial to their reputation, the treatment would in many cases constitute a breach of the artist's moral rights, even in the absence of objectively demonstrable loss. There have accordingly been very few actions concerning moral rights in the UK but they are much better known in France, notwithstanding the fact that each country is a signatory to the Berne Convention and has implemented domestic legislation to enact its provisions. This divergence owes its origins to the historical difference in the way the two countries have viewed art and its creation either as an asset or as an entirely separate phenomenon.

Another area of increasing conflict has been the balance of rights between one artist and another where an artist 'appropriates' an existing work for their own creative process or purpose. This gives rise to difficult questions over when a work is a copy of another work (and therefore a copyright infringement if lacking the original artist's consent) or when the new work becomes sufficiently original or at least transformative to stand as an original work in its own right. Instances of 'appropriation' cases ending up before the courts include a dispute between photographer Art Rodgers (1918–2011) over the use by Jeff Koons of his photograph of puppies as the basis for a similar sculpture in the US in 1989–92, or the case settled between Katrijn van Giel and Luc Tuymans (b.1958) in Belgium in 2014/15 over a painting closely based on a photograph of a Belgian politician. A similar conflict in artists' rights can arise between one artist's copyright and a second artist's right to reproduce the earlier work for caricature or parody.

The European Union addressed this issue in the engagingly so-called 'InfoSoc Directive' (Directive 2001/29) in which it grappled with the balance between the rights, duties, cultures and legal systems involved in a globalised and digitised world. While in the West it is widely accepted that the ability to use an image for a work of parody should be supported under general principles of free speech and comment, what is meant by 'parody' (so as to defeat a claim for copyright infringement) varies considerably from place to place. The question was referred in 2013/14 by the Belgian national court to the European Court of Justice, after a Belgian political party had issued a caricature of a well-known Belgian comic image in order to make a political point, and the estate of the original artist objected (Johan Deckmyn and Vrijheidsfonds VZW v Helena Vandersteen and others). The European Court attempted to identify the balance between the requirements of parody (evocation of an earlier work as an expression of humour or mockery) and the freedom of expression by the creator of the parody on the one hand, with the rights and protections afforded to the creator of the original work, on the other. The court then determined that it was for the Belgian national court to determine how that balance should be applied. Both the Directive and the European Court expressly acknowledge that – even when applying a universal EU law – national courts have a significant role in taking into account divergent traditions in assessing the balance of competing artists' rights. The UK introduced a similar approach to the parody problem in 2014, providing that parody should be treated as 'fair dealing' and not a copyright infringement, so long as it involved an imitation of a work for humorous or satirical effect (prompting the sobering thought that the defence to a copyright infringement claim in the UK might depend on the judge having a sense of humour). The US also treats parody as a form of 'fair use', although crucially in the US it seems that generally the message of the parody must refer to the underlying work, whereas this is not necessary in the UK.

Another right for artists having its roots in the French approach is the Artists' Resale Right (ARR), also known in France as the *droit de suite*. This right was originally introduced in response to situations where recognition of an artist's work does not arise until late in the artist's career or after their death, with the result that the benefits of increased value of the works of art previously sold would accrue to the current owners of the art and not to the artist. The idea that an individual could continue to benefit from sales of items for which they had freely negotiated a price and then sold is alien to common law legal systems such as those of the US and the UK, where the sale contract would have the full and final say on price and profit for the seller. Here again the French approach differs in its special treatment for art over other assets and chattels. ARR had been included under the terms of the Berne Convention but, as with moral rights, was made subject to contracting countries' own legal systems. So while California has long had an artists' resale right for transactions governed by its state law, ARR was not widely applied in legal systems not sharing the French cultural root. Following a 2001 harmonisation directive in the EU, however, the right has become law through all states of the EU, which have to provide for a sliding scale of charges on each resale in the EU by a market professional, of qualifying work by a qualifying artist, during the artist's lifetime and during the 70 years following their death. In view of the substantial legal and cultural changes this would require in the UK, that country was given additional time to implement all the provisions of the directive (relating to deceased artists), which only came into force in the UK from 1 January 2012. A different version of ARR has been implemented in Australia and an equivalent has been under consideration in the US, at least for sales at auction. Artists' resale rights – as with their freedom of expression, copyright and moral rights – remain widely divergent depending on location in spite of an increasingly globalised art world and considerable efforts to harmonise such rights around the world.

Tom Christopherson

Bibliography

Berne Convention for the Protection of Literary and Artistic Works, 9 September 1886, www.wipo.int/treaties/en/text

Brooklyn Inst. of Arts and Sciences v City of New York and Rudolph W. Giuliani, 64F. Supp. 2d 184 (EDNY 1999), and see also Prowda, *Visual Arts and the Law*, pp 31–33

Campbell v. Acuff-Rose Music, 510 U.S. 569 (1994) and Dr. Seuss Enterprises
v Penguin Books United States Court of Appeals for the Ninth Circuit,
27 March 1997

Court of Justice of the European Union in Case C-201/13 Johan Deckmyn
and Vrijheidsfonds VZW v Helena Vandersteen and others; commentary
by the 1709 Blog at http://the1709blog.blogspot.co.uk/2014/09/
parody-deckmyn-and-right-to-object-to.html

European Artists' Resale Right – Directive 2001/84/EC of the European
Parliament and of the Council of 27 September 2001 on the Resale Right
for the Benefit of the Author of an Original Work of Art at http://
eur-lex.europa.eu/legal-content/EN/ALL/?uri=CELEX:32001L0084

'The InfoSoc Directive', Directive 2001/29/EC at Recital 31, *Official Journal
L 167*, 22 June 2001, pp 10–19

Katrijn van Giel v. Luc Tuymans, Institute of Art and Law blog, http://www.ial.
uk.com/news/tag/luc-tuymans/ and Plagiarism Settlement for Luc Tuymans,
Artnet News, 2 October 2015, https://news.artnet.com>people>luc-tuymans

Parody (UK) – S.30A, Copyright, Designs and Patents Act 1988, at https://www.
gov.uk/government/uploads/system/uploads/attachment_data/file/308729/
cdpa1988-unofficial.pdf

Prowda, Judith B., *Visual Arts and the Law*, Lund Humphries in association with
Sotheby's Institute of Art, 2013

Rogers v. Koons, 960 F.2d 301 (2d Cir. 1992); Traub, James, *Art Rogers vs. Jeff
Koons*, reproduced by The Design Observer Group, at http://designobserver.
com/feature/art-rogers-vs-jeff-koons/6467

Stokes, Simon, *Art & Copyright*, Hart Publishing Ltd, 2012

Windich, Max, 'Copyright Exceptions: Fifty Shades of Parody', Penningtons
Manches, 6 October 2015 at http://www.penningtons.co.uk/news-
publications/latest-news/copyright-exceptions-–-fifty-shades-of-parody/

Whistler, James McNeill, *Eden versus Whistler: The Baronet and the Butterfly.
A Valentine with a Verdict*, Louis-Henry May, 1899

DUE DILIGENCE

'Due diligence' is generally taken to refer to the pre-contract enquiries made by a potential buyer or investor; in the context of transactions involving art, the requirement for due diligence can equally apply to potential sellers and buyers of art and is also of fundamental importance to art valuers and authenticators, as well as a range of intermediaries. Due diligence is sometimes a strict legal requirement, interwoven with the laws of title (ownership), or underpinning regulations concerning the prevention of money-laundering and the use of criminally sourced funds, as well as laws enacted for the protection of cultural and national heritage. In a more general sense, due diligence informs the work of the art authenticator seeking a second perspective to underpin or undermine their initial evaluation of a work, or the conservator considering the breadth and depth of a proposed intervention with the fabric of an object. Due diligence can also have a direct effect on a work of art's value, through uncovering either exciting or alternatively troublesome provenance, over and above those issues which would give rise to purely legal concerns. In the context of art and heritage therefore, due diligence can cover a range of related but distinct activities, depending upon the needs of the parties concerned and the circumstances of the transaction.

What is due diligence in practice? It might be more helpful to begin with a statement as to what due diligence is not. It should not be a simple and definitive list of steps or a tick-box exercise with a prescribed conclusion, although it is sometimes described as such (usually when an observer, with hindsight, judges previous efforts to have been insufficient). Rather, it represents a process whereby a series of initial questions take into account the surrounding circumstances and available information, and are intended to give rise to answers which might provoke further questions, but which might not, depending on the context. While it might start with something resembling a checklist, whether and how the process continues will depend on the experience of the person concerned and their ability to gauge whether further enquiry is required or would be justified. The process is interactive and to an extent intuitive.

In some cases, the law has set out strict requirements for due diligence and therefore has provided a basis for a legal definition for transactions in art. Following signature of the UNESCO Convention on Prohibiting and Preventing the Illicit Import, Export and Transfer of Cultural Property in 1970, some contracting states used their domestic implementation legislation to impose specific obligations of due diligence upon possessors of cultural property. The Dutch implementation of UNESCO, for instance, requires a dealer to keep an account of the parties to the transaction and the price, and requires that a stolen property register be consulted along with other relevant documentation and that appropriate enquiries into provenance should be made. Even these strict requirements are necessarily situation-specific and subject to an assessment that the possessor/acquirer of cultural property has taken all steps which a reasonable person in those circumstances would have taken.

It is therefore difficult to provide a specific and all-reaching definition for due diligence, and while it may be straightforward to identify cases where it appears that no due diligence has taken place, it is more difficult to judge the adequacy of such due diligence as was attempted. This is encapsulated in the use of the (for lawyers) loaded term 'reasonable' in the various encapsulations of due diligence. This term brings into play a balance between the subjectivity of the person concerned at the time and the objectivity of the detached observer – i.e. given who the enquirer was and what they actually knew at the time, what else should they have known or suspected, and (in the view of the observer) what enquiries should they have made? Beyond some simple initial questions, the process quickly moves away from a one-size-fits-all formula. Equally, what the researcher or the observer happens to learn after the event should not be or become part of the equation; hindsight is a precious commodity but an unfair judge.

In the context of the sale and purchase of art, a buyer's due diligence would start with enquiries about the seller's title to (ownership of) the item

– how did they obtain it and when? Does the ownership story appear to make sense? Is there independent collaboration for the story, perhaps in the form of invoices, exhibition details, insurance and shipping documentation? Further enquiries would usually include a formal search of one or more of the databases of lost and stolen art, such as maintained by the Art Loss Register, Interpol or the Art Recovery Group. Leading auction houses and art dealers conduct such searches as standard practice. Other searches (depending on the item and circumstances) might include enquiries of the police, or checking other sources such as the art press and more general publications, from the *Antiques Trade Gazette* and *The Art Newspaper* to local newspapers, for reports of thefts and losses in the relevant vicinity. If the item is, or might be considered, cultural heritage with an identifiable place of origin, is there documentation to demonstrate its lawful removal from that place, or should the local authorities be approached for confirmation? In some jurisdictions it is also possible to check against central registers for liens (lenders' security interests) that have been registered against the item where (for instance) it has been used as collateral for a financial loan; in the US for example such filings are made under the Uniform Commercial Code and can be searched. In the UK however, it is not possible to check for liens or security interests filed against works of art, unless the item happens to be owned by a company which has registered a mortgage or other debt over its assets (in which case the check would be against the name of the company and not the item). How far these matters are pursued depends on the circumstances – how valuable is the piece and how does the available information fit together; does the available information give rise to specific concerns? Is the piece uniquely identifiable, one of a known series or an item in general use; does it have distinguishing features?

On occasion, information provided or discovered should give rise to new lines of enquiry. Soil on an object of antiquity would suggest recent excavation and any provenance suggesting otherwise should be treated with considerable caution. Equally, an indication in the provenance that the work of art was in mainland Europe in the 1930s and 1940s would suggest that a potential buyer should refer to specialist looted art databases and establish a clear and reliable history of ownership for the 1933–45 period, to exclude the possibility of Nazi misappropriation or forced sale. By way of comparison, the appearance of a work of art in the hands of a known landed gentry family with historically recorded art collections might permit the researcher to take a more confident view if faced with a paucity of paperwork evidencing inheritance of an item. This is indicative of an underlying obstacle encountered in due diligence activities for works of art. There is no general requirement that ownership of chattels be registered or dispositions recorded, and there may simply be no record of previous ownership or transfer for many items. This is not in itself inherently suspicious. Objects of lesser value, or those which have only acquired value more recently through usage or survival, may not have left their mark on history and may have limited provenance. However, the lack of paperwork in one case might be of more concern than in another, and the obligation (and skill) of the art researcher is to judge when further research is necessary and will bear fruit and where it is not and will not; the general requirement is, after all, to undertake *reasonable* due diligence. Similar due diligence processes come into play in cases of questioned attribution and authenticity. While the primary role of the authenticator will be concerned with the examination of the object itself, the examination of its provenance may provide vital information supporting or undermining the object in question. In particular, a lack of provable provenance beyond a certain point may lead to questions about recent re-attributions and discoveries, as seen for instance in the continuing debate about the attribution to Leonardo da Vinci of the so-called *La Bella Principessa*, where documented provenance to date only appears to reach back to 1998 (see 'Authenticity'). Art forgers, unfortunately, are equally aware of the importance of provenance and in several high-profile forgery cases, such as Drewe/Myatt and Greenhalgh (see pp 101–2 and 110), the creation of false provenance has been as important as the creation of the forged art. This was particularly prominent with the Beltracchi forgeries of the 1990s, where an entire art collection was invented (the so-called 1920s Sammlung Jägers or Jaegers), with records, exhibition labels, photographic evidence and authenticity certificates created to support the forged art works. These examples underpin the importance of effective due diligence in the authentication process and point to the difficulties in reducing the due diligence process to a checklist or series of defined steps. As soon as the authenticator adheres to a prescribed format the forger can reproduce the material required to satisfy the needs of that format. Due diligence, in this field as in others, retains the need for a questioning approach, an experienced eye and a degree of intuition.

Due diligence can have a direct influence over legal title to an item (the right to enjoy unrestricted ownership of it). In many cases, the degree of due diligence undertaken by a prospective buyer will be an important factor in determining whether or not they are deemed to be a buyer 'in good faith'. This in turn influences the extent to which they obtain a superior legal title against a wrongly dispossessed former owner. In many civil law jurisdictions, such as Italy, a buyer in good faith is deemed to have acquired good title from the time of purchase, as against any claims by earlier owners who had been wrongfully dispossessed of the item. In France on the other hand, the purchaser is deemed to have acquired superior title to a dispossessed claimant after three years from a good faith purchase – and good faith is assumed unless the dispossessed claimant can prove otherwise. Jurisdictions such as the UK are more protective towards the original owner by providing that the wrongful possessor of an item (such as a thief) cannot ever acquire title to it and neither, in principle, can anyone acquiring the object from that wrongful possessor. This was historically described by the legal dictum *Nemo dat quod non habet*, which provides that no one can pass (title) that they do not themselves hold, and is now enshrined in the Sale of Goods Act 1979. The different approaches were examined by the English courts in Winkworth v Christie Manson and Woods, where a good faith buyer of netsuke carvings in Italy was deemed to have good title under Italian law, and so defeated (in the English courts) the claim of the original (English) owner from whom the carvings had been originally stolen, even though English law would have preferred a timely claim by the original owner in the event that the good faith purchase following the theft had been made in England.

However, even the UK will protect the title of a good faith purchaser against competing title claims made more than six years after their purchase of the item, so long as that purchase can be shown to have been made in good faith. In contrast to France, in the UK it is for the subsequent owner to prove that they did buy in good faith, as this is not assumed. Accordingly, both in countries operating civil law and common law systems, proof of reasonable due diligence prior to purchase is an important part of any subsequent determination of whether the purchase was made in good faith, in order to qualify for the protections referenced above. While the level of required due diligence in such cases is sometimes specified in law (for instance for dealers in Switzerland) it is not always so. The *absence* of due diligence, however, always raises the suspicion that the purchase was not in good faith, and therefore opens the door for a competing title claim at a later date. This is particularly the case where the purchaser is a dealer or art world *savant*, who ought to know better, or where the circumstances of the particular transaction suggest that further questions should have been asked.

Due diligence has also become a requirement of good practice through the requirements of various codes of practice and ethics. Early examples include the adoption by museums and museum associations of due diligence guidelines for the acquisition of cultural artefacts, in response to the 1970 UNESCO Convention on Prohibiting and Preventing the Illicit Import, Export and Transfer of Cultural Property. The Convention provides a framework for contracting states to prohibit the importation of cultural property stolen from museums or archaeological sites or cultural property illegally exported from contracting states and encompasses the need for the institutions of contracting states to identify and return objects illicitly acquired after the date of the Convention. Over and above the strict legal requirements contained in countries' implementation legislation referenced above, this led to the development of policy and ethical requirements for pre-acquisition due diligence, to ensure that artefacts illicitly traded after 1970 were not finding their way into museum collections. These museum codes marked the beginning of a substantial change in museum and market practice, which hitherto had tended to focus upon the laws of the state in which an acquisition was being made, at the expense of detailed investigation into the circumstances and rules governing the previous history of the object and its arrival in that state. Establishing back story of the artefact and its journey from source to ultimate acquisition therefore became an integral part of the final acquisition process. For example, the Code of Ethics for the Museums Association in the UK requires member museums to 'perform due diligence checks to ensure that there is no suspicion that since 1970 [the date of the Convention] the item might have been exported, acquired, sold, illegally excavated or removed from a monument, site or wreck or otherwise transferred in contravention of: UK law . . . the law of the country of origin . . . [or] international law and conventions on the protection or export of cultural property'.

A common requirement of the museum codes of practice on both sides of the Atlantic is that museums should only deal with those engaged in the cultural property trade who adopt similar standards, and in due course codes of practice matching those adopted by the museums have been taken up by the leading dealers and auction houses. The most high-profile of these in the UK was the 'Due Diligence Code for Dealers Trading in Fine Art, Antiques, Antiquarian Books, Manuscripts and Collectors' Items' issued by the Council for the Prevention of Art Theft (COPAT) in 1999; auction houses such as Sotheby's and Christie's have also adopted their own codes of ethics and business conduct, appropriate to their international businesses. The development of the various codes of practice for the acquisition of items of cultural importance since 1970 has made due diligence into provenance and export history for such items integral to the process of sale and purchase. There have been similar developments relating to the movement for the effective restitution of Nazi looted art, encapsulated by the 'Washington Principles on Nazi-Confiscated Art' adopted at the Washington Congress in 1998. A consequence is that due diligence to establish clean provenance has become a requirement of both museums and other potential purchasers, who require assurance against the taint of previous illegal excavation, export, dispossession or sale. Good provenance and the fruits of due diligence have therefore grown to have a direct and significant effect on desirability, saleability and value of the objects concerned.

The laws of many countries also make forms of due diligence a mandatory requirement of certain transactions as a part of the international drive to combat money-laundering and the use of the proceeds of crime. Whereas the due diligence described above mainly concerns the object, due diligence in this area primarily concerns the individuals concerned in the transaction and the source of the funds being used. Various studies have suggested that commerce in moveable and sometimes untraceable art and cultural objects is particularly attractive to those seeking to convert the proceeds of crime (be it from theft, looting, illegal excavation, drug and arms trafficking or tax evasion) into untainted funds that are usable around the world. There have been, for instance, widespread reports of sales of excavated antiquities by so-called Islamic State (Daesh) to fund their operations in Syria and Iraq. Those involved as intermediaries or sellers and buyers in the art world are therefore on notice of the need to avoid unwitting involvement with such activities and to exercise reasonable due diligence in this regard. The level of due diligence requirements under anti-money-laundering and associated regulations varies by locality. It is also determined by the type of transaction involved and the nature of parties concerned, with certain regulated institutions such as banks and financial institutions subject to greater obligations. Nevertheless, at a universal level, required due diligence is based around notions that parties should ensure they ascertain, and keep records of, the identities of their counterparties, and that they should make confidential reports to appropriate authorities of transactions they consider suspicious. 'Suspicion' can come in many forms and, as with other aspects of due diligence, is circumstance-specific. Matters potentially giving rise to suspicion (sometimes known as 'red flags') might include the payment of large amounts of cash thus circumventing the official banking system, selling prices that seem surprisingly low, transactions that have to be conducted in a great rush without apparent reason, or the introduction of complicated steps in a transaction that appear to have no explanation. Additional due diligence requirements apply when there is the potential for dealing with 'politically sensitive persons' – such as government and ruling officials and their close families – to guard against involvement (unwitting or otherwise) in the proceeds of corruption. In many jurisdictions, including the EU and the US, the failure to conduct adequate due diligence in situations where money-laundering appears to be a risk, and failure to report suspicious transactions, constitute a criminal offence.

Due diligence therefore forms an important aspect of a wide range of activities in the art world, and is a significant factor underpinning issues of authenticity, ownership, ethical practice and potential criminal sanction. However, the need for due diligence in such a wide range of circumstances and to fulfil such varied roles, with the inherent uncertainty around what constitutes 'due' diligence from one case to another, means that for the art world this will continue to be an umbrella term for a range of processes and judgements, not easily reduced to a cleanly definable abstract principle or set of requirements.

Tom Christopherson

Bibliography

1970 UNESCO Convention on Prohibiting and Preventing the Illicit Import, Export and Transfer of Ownership of Cultural property (Implementation) Act, 12 July 2009, http://www.wetten.nl (Article 87 a); trans. in English: http://www.unesco.org/culture/natlaws/media/pdf/netherlands/netherlands_implementationact_conv1970_engtof.pdf

Beltracchi forgeries; The Jaegers Collection, see http://alfredflechtheim.com/en/reception/the-jaegers-collection/

Christie's Corporate Social Responsibility, http://www.christies.com/about-us/corporate-social-responsibility

'Due Diligence Code for Dealers Trading in Fine Art, Antiques, Antiquarian Books, Manuscripts and Collectors' Items', Council for the Prevention of Art Theft (COPAT), http://www.aba.org.uk/About-the-ABA/ABA-Rules-Guidelines/Advice-to-Members/Due-Diligence-CoPAT-Code

'Due diligence is necessary to underpin a purchase in good faith': De Préval v Adrian Alan Limited [1997] QBD (unreported), France v Williams 4 June 1999 Bull. Crim. (Audience Publique): Cass. Crim, 4 June 1999, Bull.Crim.(Arrêt Schloss)

'Good faith purchaser under Italian law acquires title (even in the English courts)', Winkworth v Christie Manson and Woods [1980] 1 All ER

LOOTED ART DATABASES

www.artloss.com/en; www.lootedart.com; www.lostart.de/Webs/DE/Start/Index.html

Einsatzstab Reichsleiter Rosenberg (ERR), the Nazi Taskforce for collecting looted art, see http://art.claimscon.org/our-work/records-of-the-einsatzstab-reichsleiter-rosenberg-err/

The Munich Central Collecting Point Archive records are now located at the US National Gallery of Art, www.nga.gov/resources/dpamunich.shtm

Le Répertoire des Biens Spoliés en France Durant la Guerre 1939–1945, http://www.culture.gouv.fr/documentation/mnr/MnR-rbs.htm#

'Museums Association Acquisition Guidance on the Ethics and Practicalities of Acquisition', *Ethical Guidelines*, 2004, no.1, 2nd edn, para 4.2

'Principles of conduct of the UK art market', adopted by members of the British Art Market Federation (BAMF), http://tbamf.org.uk/portfolio/bamf-principles-of-conduct/

Prowda, Judith B., *Visual Arts and the Law*, Lund Humphries in association with Sotheby's Institute of Art, 2013

'Right to reclaim stolen goods in England is indefinite as against the thief and their associates, but is extinguished after 6 years after a good faith purchase', Limitation Act 1980, s 4

'Sale of Goods Act 1979', ss 12 and 21, http://www.legislation.gov.uk/ukpga/1979/54

'Sotheby's Code of Business Conduct', pp 50-51, www.sothebys.com/content/dam/sothebys/PDFs/JC_1416483_Legal_Code%20of%20Conduct%20Brochure.pdf.

'Washington Principles on Nazi-Confiscated Art', www.state.gov/p/eur/rt/hlcst/122038.htm

BUYING AND SELLING

THE AUCTION PROCESS

Unlike the commercial gallery, the art auction offers a degree of transparency with its ostensibly public financial transactions. Auction results have therefore become a socially acceptable definition of the financial value as well as ownership of the art object. Despite appearing open to all, however, the auction remains a complex process of social actions and interactions requiring specialist knowledge as well as risk management. Art auctions differ from other auctions in that each commodity is unique, and therefore an absolute 'eternal' value can never be established: the value of each work can only be defined by what an individual was prepared to pay for it at the time of the auction. That resulting financial value is, nevertheless, greatly influenced by the manner in which the work is presented and marketed by the auction house, as well as by the psychological understanding and 'control' of bidders' behaviour by the auctioneer. Indeed, the final auction price can have a tremendous effect on the fame of the artist and their subsequent prices at both auction and in private treaty sales.

The international world of fine art auctions is dominated by two brand names, Sotheby's and Christie's. In spite of recent inroads into the market share by Chinese auction houses, the duopoly still accounts for 40–50 per cent of global annual auction turnover. Since their origins in eighteenth-century London, they have grown into multinational corporations with sales rooms and offices worldwide. Christie's and Sotheby's have the lion's share of the international market for fine art, while other international metropolitan and regional auction houses are better known for their sales of local contemporary art, decorative art, collectibles and niche sectors. The notion of the fine art auction as a glamorous evening event was constructed in 1958 by Peter Wilson (1913–84), Chairman of Sotheby's from 1957 to 1980, when, for the first time, a black-tie sale of seven impressionist and post-impressionist paintings took place in front of VIP guests and TV cameras.

The function of the auction house is to act as an agent for the tertiary resale of art objects. The auctioneer's prime responsibility is to attain the highest price on behalf of the consignor. Today, the major auction houses have encroached on the traditional role of the dealer, providing a range of art investment advisory services to their 'preferred' clients. For example, in recent years both Christie's and Sotheby's have acquired several existing commercial galleries together with their stocks of art objects, which have then been offered for sale. This extends to contemporary art: the most famous example being the *Beautiful Inside My Head Forever* single-artist sale of 2008, in which the artist Damien Hirst circumvented his dealers and sold new work directly through Sotheby's in London (see 'Artist–Dealer Relationships'). Sotheby's has also established an annual sale of large-scale high-end sculptures at Chatsworth House in Derbyshire, the home of the Devonshire family. Many of these works are commissioned or being sold for the first time. The cultural and monetary value of these works is boosted by their display, although there is no eventual auction. In common with art dealers, potential buyers negotiate prices in private, and Sotheby's ensures that the sculptures end up in respected private or corporate art collections, in order to strengthen their future provenance value. Christie's imitated Sotheby's in 2013 by launching a similar sculptural display in the grounds of Waddesdon House in Buckinghamshire, home of the Rothschild family.

The auction process begins when the owner of an art object decides to sell it and becomes the 'consignor'. Most sales and resales of art at auction tend to be a consequence of 'the three Ds' – debt, divorce and death. In many countries, the estate will incur inheritance (or estate) tax, compelling beneficiaries to liquidate part of the estate. During this process of appraisal and valuation, the consignor will often solicit the opinion of more than one auction house and/or dealers before deciding on the best place to sell: at this point, auction houses will often attempt to win the consignment by offering a *douceur*. This can include lowering, or sometimes even waiving, the consignor's commission on any future sale; and, in the case of high-end works, guaranteeing a minimum price to the consignor, which is paid by the auction house if the work fails to sell, or sells but falls short of the guarantee. The guarantee presents a risk to the auction house, and is therefore usually underwritten by a third party, who consequently benefits from a share of the commission in a successful sale.

Once a work has been consigned to an auction house, the cataloguing process begins. The catalogue is an important marketing tool, and illustrative exposure on the front, back and inside covers is considered prime. The early pages of the catalogue include the name and date of the sale, together with dates for the exhibition (preview), and a list of specialists. The final pages contain the 'small print' that includes important information regarding registration, taxes and conditions of sale. The main body of the catalogue comprises the objects in order of sale, and each catalogue entry provides a colour photograph and detailed description of the object, including the lot number, name and dates of the artist, and title of the work. This is followed by the work's physical and documentary qualities, including medium, signature and position, size and production date. There follows the estimated price, ranging from low to high estimate. Provenance, exhibition and literature details are accompanied by expert discussion of the formal and contextual qualities of the work, known as the 'catalogue note'.

The provenance lists the ownership history of the object in chronological order from its production to the present day. If a modern work, it will typically include the artist's primary dealer, followed by other galleries which have acquired the work on the secondary market, as well as dates when the work appeared at auction. Negative auction results are omitted, and prospective buyers should always check the work's sales history on auction databases. The provenance list will typically finish with a statement such as 'Acquired from the above by the family of the present owner(s) in 1936' or 'Purchased at the above sale by the present owner(s)' or, as in this case, 'Thence by descent to the present owner(s)'. The quality of the provenance, and the relative frequency of a change in ownership, can have a profound effect on the market value of the object. For example, if the work has never appeared on the market, or has not appeared for the last 25 years, it is considered to be relatively under-exposed, and therefore likely to prove more attractive to potential buyers. Works that have frequently changed hands, say every ten years or so, are far less attractive to buyers. 'Good provenance' can also include works that have been in alpha galleries and/or important collections. For obvious reasons, international contemporary art is likely to have a shorter provenance history, but the same rules apply. The primary gallery is a crucial marker of 'good provenance'. In many jurisdictions the law demands auction houses pursue due diligence (see 'Due Diligence') when appraising consigned art. Auction houses are under particular pressure to investigate the provenance of art obtained from owners and traders in German-occupied Europe between 1933 and 1945.

Contemporary work that appears too quickly at auction should be treated with caution. Premature appearance at auction is an ambiguous sign: the artist might be rapidly gaining in value, with demand outstripping supply, and therefore the owner might be hoping to profit from the surge of interest; on the other hand, they might be trying to offload a work with no investment future. This regularly happens with immoveable gallery stock in all art market sectors. There are no failsafe criteria in judging provenance. Sometimes works that appear to have an unattractive provenance will sell well for other reasons, including changes of fashion, a new appraisal of the work as a 'sleeper', or that it has been undervalued in previous market transactions because of a failure to assess its quality or to identify the artist. A famous example from 2008 was a glass crystal ewer, which was catalogued by a provincial English auction house as 'a nineteenth-century French claret jug' with an estimate of just $130–$265. To the delight of the consignor, it sold for $290,000, only to reappear at Christie's, London and to sell for $4.22 million. During this time the 'sleeper' jug had been correctly identified as an extremely rare tenth- or eleventh-century Fatimid ewer. Because of the controversy caused by the failure to correctly identify the object, the initial sale had been annulled, and all parties, including the first vendor and purchaser, came to a confidential agreement to reoffer the work at the subsequent Christie's sale, sharing in the profits.

The exhibition history of an art object at auction can also have a positive effect on its value, especially if this includes public exhibition as well as display in commercial galleries. The frequency and quality of these exhibitions is a clear marker of both the commercial and academic validation of the object and may also demonstrate whether the work is of local, national or international interest to dealers and museum curators. The exhibition and display history often expanded upon in the catalogue note can be eloquent concerning the proactive marketing of certain types of art created in limited multiple editions, as well as unique art objects which nevertheless are similar to others by the same artist. In the case of Old Master paintings in particular, the catalogue description often refers to a 'similar' work held in an important museum collection, thus marketing the auction lot by means of 'reflected glory'; the implication is that by purchasing the work, you might own something of 'museum quality'. The catalogue entry of limited-edition works for sale such as bronze sculptures or photographs will often list other examples of the edition held in public or private collections. The literature section also serves to validate the work, by demonstrating whether it has been considered worthy enough to be included in both private and public exhibition catalogues as well as academic publications. Literature entries are particularly impressive if they include illustrations of the work, indicative of its particular importance in the *oeuvre* of the artist. In this section the catalogue raisonné will also be listed, providing further validation of the work. The catalogue note, also referred to as the description, can range from no description in day sale catalogues, to several paragraphs or even pages for the more important evening sales. The larger auctions are divided between an evening sale of a relatively small number of more important works, and the day sale, with a much larger volume of lesser works, often by the same artists as represented in the evening sale. Evening sales are often glamorous social events with invited guests, whilst the day sale tends to be less crowded and formal. Catalogue descriptions will often include further illustrations of the work, such as archive photographs of the artist in their studio, together with comparative images of other related art objects.

The number of lots in any particular auction will vary for different reasons. In a typical evening sale there could be between 40 and 70 works, whilst the lesser-value day sale will include between 120 and 180 works. The lots may be previewed at their associated exhibition, which usually begins four or five days prior to the actual sale. Because of the tight scheduling of auctions, the exhibitions often include weekend openings, facilitating the viewing of works of art during the non-working day. Significant works of art will be sent on an international tour of major art market centres such as New York, Paris and Hong Kong. This is a complicated logistical operation requiring high-security transportation and attendant costs, but is considered worth the time and expenses incurred because of the high profile gained in marketing terms. Works of art within the catalogue are strategically placed. In order to strike a key note at the start of the auction, the first lot is always selected to catch audience interest, be it visually and/or in terms of its rarity, commerciality or contextuality. Lot 1 is rarely of high value, and is usually deliberately under-estimated in order to create early buyer confidence. The first five or six lots tend to be appetisers that prepare the audience for an important piece placed between lots 7 and 10. The positioning of 'star lots' varies from sale to sale, but usually they are preceded by a lesser work by the same artist, a work by an artist of the same nationality, or a work with a similar subject. Auction houses are aware of the intelligence of their audience, and the entertainment value of the auctioneer and the auction itself, and generally attempt to avoid predictability. The final lots of a sale are the hardest to sell. Many bidders will have left the sale during the anti-climax which can follow the auction of the 'star lot'. On occasion a 'star lot' will be the final lot, as happened successfully at the Old Master and British Paintings Evening Sale at Sotheby's, London, in July 2010, when the oil painting of *Modern Rome – Campo Vaccino* (1839) by J.M.W. Turner sold for $46.03 million, doubling its low estimate. When the market is depressed, auction houses will reduce the number of lots in order to ensure reasonable turnover and to limit the 'bought in' rate of works that fail to sell. They will focus on the high end of the market because this portion tends to remain unaffected by economic downturns. Low and middle market art objects sell less well during a recession.

The auction itself is intended to be a dramatic and unpredictable event. It is never certain which works will sell for a good price or not at all, and this can create a tense and sometimes electric atmosphere. The auctioneer stands on a podium with assistants at his or her side. Portable lots are traditionally displayed as they come up for sale; larger works are sold 'as seen'. Purpose-built auction houses, such as Sotheby's, New York, have electric carousels that display the lots mechanically. A plasma screen at the front of the room above the auctioneer's head displays the current lot price in the major global currencies. To the right of the room lie banks of telephones over which poise auction house staff bidding on behalf of clients who instruct. The 'audience' consists of rows of seated dealers and private collectors who form the bulk of those bidding in the room. At major auctions, the room will be packed with buyers, sellers, the press and observers. The auction commences with a brief legal statement from the auctioneer referring to the general rules and regulations of the sale. The auctioneer introduces the first lot, and announces an opening bid. This will be somewhere below the reserve price, the amount agreed with the consignor as being the minimum they are prepared to accept for the work. The reserve price remains undisclosed, but will never be higher than the low estimate as cited in the catalogue. The auctioneer, however, will often indicate when the reserve price has been reached, with a comment such as 'I can sell'. The auctioneer has a confidential logbook in which absentee (or commission) bids are recorded; it is the auctioneer's responsibility to bid on behalf of absentees until their maximum bids are surpassed by bidders in the room, on the phone or internet. Live online internet bidding is now available in most sales via the auction house websites.

The auctioneer will continue to take bids at increments of approximately 10 per cent of the previous bid until the last bidder, known as the under-bidder, drops out. At this point the auctioneer will announce that he or she is going to sell, and give fair warning before finally bringing the hammer down on the podium. The auctioneer will then announce how much the lot has sold for, and move on to the next lot. If the lot fails to achieve its reserve price, auctioneers will discreetly announce 'not sold' or 'pass'. Such unsold works are referred to as 'bought in', and these will often be sold subsequent to the auction by private treaty if the consignor is willing to accept the offer of a post-sale buyer. Bought-in works can prove difficult to sell at future auctions, and it is common to see such works appearing in a different auction house and/or in a different location.

Both the consignor and the purchaser at auction have to pay a commission, also known as the premium. For the consignor, this amount is not published but is normally around 10 per cent of the hammer price, although this commission can be waived if the consignor is a regular or VIP client. The buyer's commission is listed at the back of every auction catalogue, and can vary from house to house, with the bigger names generally charging more. Most auction houses have tapered commissions. For example, Bonhams, Christie's and Sotheby's worldwide currently charge (2015): 25 per cent of the hammer price for the first $65,000; 20 per cent for $65,000 to $1.3 million; and 12 per cent for anything higher. Smaller auction houses generally offer significantly lower commissions in order to remain competitive.

There are other extra costs of which the buyer in particular needs to be aware. These are listed in the 'small print' at the back of all auction catalogues and include import and export duties and other taxes. There are different national and international import and export rates, including specific rates for transactions in the European Union. Symbols relating to any applicable special taxes appear beside the catalogue estimate for every work. For example a double dagger signifies that import duties must be paid as the work has been imported from outside of the European Union. A recent extra charge in the United Kingdom is the Artist's Resale Right, also referred to as *droit de suite*. This acknowledges that the living artist, or the estate of an artist up to 70 years following his death, has a continuing right to his creation and merits a proportion of its repeated resale income. The cross within a circle symbol signifies the Resale Royalty Right payable to the artist. Like the buyer's commission, this forms a tapering percentage of the hammer price, currently around 4 per cent with a maximum liability of $14,230. The Artist's Resale Right applies throughout the EU, but does not apply in the US. With all these added extras, a buyer will end up paying an additional 30 per cent on top of the hammer price for a work by a contemporary artist, along with any applicable VAT and/or import/export taxes.

Auction houses offer assistance with transportation arrangements, but the costs remain the responsibility of the buyer. Sold lots are paid for and, if portable, taken by their buyers within the next 24 hours, or they are removed to a warehouse in transit to an international airport. It is remarkable that a significant number of such warehoused works are neglected by their buyers, and can remain unclaimed for years.

David Bellingham

Bibliography

Adam, Georgina, *Big Bucks: The Explosion of the Art Market in the 21st Century*,
Lund Humphries, 2014, ch.1, pp 214–5

Bench, Aleya, *Appraising Art*, Hudson Hills Press, 2013

Harvey, Brian, and Franklin Meisel, *Auctions Law and Practice*, Oxford University Press, 2006, 3rd edn

Lacey, Robert, *Sotheby's: Bidding for Class*, Sphere, 1999

Leab, Daniel J., and Katharine Kyes Leab, *The Auction Companion*,
Harper Collins, 1981

Smith, Charles W., *Auctions: The Social Construction of Value*,
University of California, 1992

Stefanick, Frank, *Inside the Auction Game*, 1st Book Library, 1991

ART FAIRS

Art fairs, like tennis tournaments, are graded according to their level of significance. There are strict conditions for entry to the art world's grand slams that appear to favour Western blue-chip dealers. The two most venerable are the oldest, Art Basel (est. 1970) and the European Fine Art Fair (TEFAF) in Maastricht (originally founded as the Pictura Art Fair, est. 1987). The major-league additions, Art Basel Miami Beach (est. 2002), Art Basel Hong Kong (est. 2013), Frieze, which opened in London in 2003 and Frieze New York and Masters (est. 2011), comprise the gilded clutch. You need to be a dealer in the top 300 to stand a chance of being selected for the main draw. Art Basel, the largest, offers a space to 280 dealers, who together exhibit the work of over 4,000 artists. Strict vetting and selection processes are put in place by the fair organisers. TEFAF operates a rigorous authentication process as one of its founding principles was that 'vetting should be more rigorous than at any existing fair and as far as possible should be conducted by outside experts rather than exhibitors'. The list of vetters includes curators from the Rijksmuseum, the Mauritshuis, the Frick Collection, the Getty, the National Gallery of Art in Washington, the British Museum, the Victoria and Albert Museum, the Hermitage and the Louvre. However, many other fairs, notably those focusing on international contemporary art, do not have a vetting committee, including Frieze and more surprisingly Art Basel, in which 70 per cent of the dealers are primary, instead they operate a selection committee comprising an international make-up of dealers. The Art Show, organised by the Art Dealers Association of America, another without a committee, insists, by way of a defence, that all its members comply with the association's code of ethics. Once a dealer secures a booth in one of the grand slam fairs, they are able to sell art at the highest level. The second-tier fair (tennis Masters events) often has regional importance but, bar a few highlights, shows art without an international pedigree. The satellite art fair circuit, which counts among its events the Affordable Art Fair in London, can seem superfluous because in the main it comprises art that mimics the international contemporary art aesthetic.

It is the grand slam events that catch the art world's attention. When Art Basel first declared its acquisition of a 60 per cent stake in Art Hong Kong and when Frieze announced that it would be setting up a New York arm to its London event, the market was energised, although the impact on the market is now viewed by many as a transmogrification because the mergers have created a fair super-brand, where once there were merely cavernous spaces in which dealers plied their trade. In the world of fine art and antiques, TEFAF is not in direct competition with Masterpiece (est. 2010), although on the surface it may appear otherwise. Its predecessor, the Grosvenor House Art and Antiques Fair, which closed in 2009, and which Masterpiece ostensibly replaced, was aimed at European collectors of the decorative arts. Both fairs attract an eclectic array of dealers to bring a great range of material to the events and demand high rental fees for large stands. The works of art for sale in Masterpiece appeal to an extremely wealthy, largely non-European elite, resident in London, although it has the flavour of Art Palm Beach, with the audience possibly less specialist than those attending other specific fine art or design fairs. The revived Olympia Fine Art and Antiques Fair (est. 1973) and the smaller and exclusive Art Antiques, London (est. 1989) together provide home-grown competition for Masterpiece, because they concentrate on the decorative arts and fine art respectively, two categories of art that Masterpiece represents under one roof.

Art Basel, Frieze and TEFAF, each pre-eminent in its field, cover in effect the four most recognisable categories of art: modern, international contemporary, Old Masters and high-end antiques (particularly Chinese) respectively. A dealer can realise 70 per cent of sales at a major international fair. The fair formula has enabled dealers to retain their approximately 50 per cent share of the global art market in spite of the incursion of auction houses into the international contemporary component of their business. Art Basel is now represented on three continents. This rationalisation of the modern and blue-chip contemporary art markets has prompted the company to represent a proportional number of alpha dealers on their respective native continents, in consideration of their national rather than international pedigree. There will of course be international uber-alpha galleries like Gagosian and Hauser & Wirth present in each leg, but the principle of pan-continental significance over an international standard is now a market reality. This is in line with the assumption that the art world has divided along three trading meridians: continental America, Asia and Europe/Middle East. The introduction of new alpha galleries from emerging markets into the pre-eminent international art fair is an acknowledgement from the heart of the trade that taste is discrepant in different places and societies. The market already replaces Western moderns with Chinese in Art Hong Kong and Western blue-chip contemporary with South American equivalents in Miami. This suggests that cultural values and perceptions have changed. Abu Dhabi Art (est. 2007 under the name Art Paris Abu Dhabi) and Istanbul Contemporary (est. 1995) already reflect, through their choice of dealers, art from the region. These fairs in particular demand that outsiders conform to the host's cultural expectations. This cultural aware-ness, which is on occasion acute, is a combination of political sensitivity (which in emerging markets prohibits variously: anti-government, anti-religious and overtly sexual imagery) and enhanced national and regional competition.

Art Basel is made more potent, ironically, by the decline of Europe's national and regional art fairs. Its triumph is a reflection of the declining economic fortunes of southern Europe and, it would appear, the concomitant rise of Germany and its near neighbours. One case in point of this decline is Spain's ARCO (est. 1982). At its peak the fair attracted an esti-mated 250,000 visitors – even though a majority of the guests were onlookers rather than buyers, in common with most international events – but it no longer draws in these audience numbers. Today, South American collectors stay away in expectation, most probably, of Art Basel Miami. Works are priced in the main at a medium level and Spanish dealers account for nearly half the representatives – the next most prominent being the influential German trade. The Spanish art market is certainly not inac-tive, in spite of the downturn of the country's economy and severe cuts to museum purchasing budgets. There are pockets of wealth in enclaves like Marbella, where enterprising dealers sell contemporary art in all its forms to wealthy Spaniards and expatriates living in La Zagaleta. However, these small outposts of prosperity are not enough to help the national market. Turin's Artissima (est. 1983), which shows 'experimental' art in the main, and Arte Fiera in Bologna (est. 1974), which showcases Italian talent from creative centres like Naples, are vulnerable to a decline in the fortunes of northern Italian collectors. Arte Fiera, perhaps aware that the national market is shrinking, has entered into a joint venture with the Shanghai fair ShContemporary (founded as the Shanghai Art Fair in 1997) and as such may be one of the few enterprising European and American brands to survive. Art fair franchises do not just take effect at grand slams. The major Paris-based Foire Internationale d'Art Contemporain (est. 1974) has expanded to Los Angeles. Paris Photo (est. 1997), the pre-eminent fine art photography fair, has also established a base in the Californian city and is active in Shanghai as well.

The marginalisation of Art Athena in Athens is very likely given the weakness of the Greek economy and the power of the Istanbul fairs. Meanwhile in emerging markets, regional and national fairs like ShContemporary and the oldest art fair in Asia, Art Taipei (est. 1993), are gaining in strength and reputation. They are now on the international collector's map. The Korea International Art Fair (est. 2001) has been outmanoeuvred and outmuscled by Art Basel Hong Kong and ShContemporary. Another art fair on the Korean peninsula, in the southern coastal town of Kwangju, has drawn together a very strong collection of international, regional and national dealers for the first time in South Korea. Art Kwangju's focus is broad and compelling, with a concentration on new media and not-for-profit spaces. With the support of the city's local government it has carved a niche for itself. The ambition of this small South Korean fair to act as a bridge between the market and world of art has become a feature, to a greater or lesser extent, of most art fairs today. Frieze Projects and Scope Basel commission artists to create site-specific works of art within and around the fair. One of the most memorable of these installations was *City of Art* by Simon Fujiwara (b.1982), in which the artist created a spoof archaeological dig inside the main tent during Frieze, London in 2010. All fairs now run educational programmes to which art world commentators and art market operators are invited to voice their views. In 2016 Artissima had the novel idea of inviting dealers to curate solo exhibitions of artists who had missed the cut. It was an intriguing initiative because it brought into stark comparison the values of the art world and those of the marketplace. The artists themselves had worked diligently throughout their lives, and in an avant-garde vein, but they had failed to advance their commercial careers, although their work was very plausible and equal to the art of other artists who had proved to be economically successful. The purpose of these seemingly uncommercial ventures is to raise the art-world credentials of the fairs, rather in the way that alpha galleries curate non-selling exhibitions. The symbolic capital that this accrues, although less significant than that garnered from a biennale, is nevertheless priceless. The formation of an art collection is a complex endeavour far more dependent on cultural confidence than on the act of procurement.

London may be the centre of the Old Master market and have, with Paris, the most diverse collection of specialist dealers in the world, but it is in the provincial town of Maastricht that the business of selling an estimated $5.65 billion of stock takes place at TEFAF. The joy of TEFAF is that it allows the collector to see material they normally would not. It also serves to restore the imbalance in representation and price between fine and decorative art and paintings, drawings and sculpture. Art Basel specialises in modern and post-war contemporary categories of the highest quality. An archetypal work by Jean-Michel Basquiat (1960–88) such as *Jack Johnson* (1982) will find its place beside a rare Andy Warhol, *One Hundred and Fifty Multicoloured Marilyns* (1963), the Arte Povera Movement (1967–72) can be shown next to that of the Gutai group (1954–72), and the world's leading galleries will display the best work that they have in stock. The collector can be presented with a litany of fine art offerings: a painting by Lucio Fontana (1899–1968), *Concetto Spaziale, Attese* (1959), at Acquavella, New York together with a charcoal on steel work, *Untitled* (1991), by Jannis Kounellis (b.1936) with Kewenig Galerie, Berlin. The Mono-ha (School of Things, 1968–75) artist Lee U-fan (b.1938) can be found at Kukje Gallery, South Korea, while Andreas Gursky's photographs might be represented by London-based White Cube Gallery. Alternative points of interest such as a 1971 version of the 1925 *Red and Blue Chair* by Gerrit Rietveld and a series of coloured drawings by Cao Fei (b.1978) on display in the up-and coming Vitamin Creative Space of Guangzhou add flavour to the first-rate fair. Outlier art like the woodblock prints of Nilima Sheikh (b.1945) might also be found, represented by a gallery like the Mumbai-based Chemould Prescott Road Gallery.

Istanbul Contemporary (est. 1995) is perhaps the most intriguing of the new challengers. Istanbul, Turkey's largest metropolis, has grown in size to 20 million residents. A procrustean political environment has cast a shadow over an art world that favours individualism, but, by dint of a coterie of significant collectors, the city is a thriving art centre, and the Turkish galleries and their wares are testimony to a resurgent and feisty contemporary culture. Many indigenous dealers like Canaan Gallery and Galerist as well as international dealers such as Rose Issa Projects focus on the craft element inherent in the work of art. Istanbul Contemporary also provides a refuge and platform for many of the galleries from North Africa, the Levant and the Middle East.

Art fairs today offer as much and more than biennales. They provide the exhilaration of the marketplace, the thrill of celebrity-spotting and the quality of museums. They offer the visitor outsized catalogues sans commentaries. It could be said that the Venice Biennale is a prelude to the consumer fest of Art Basel. Fairs reflect the cultural and collecting strength of regions rather than nations. The internationalist model pursued by Art Basel and Frieze, which is expedient, is faced with competition from the introspective art worlds of Istanbul, Taipei and Seoul, which cater for regional taste rather than offering a generic commodity to a transglobal elite.

Iain Robertson

Bibliography

Art Basel Miami Beach, Miami, 2008–10

Art Basel, Basel, 2008–12

Baratta, Paolo et al., *Illuminations, 54th International Art Exhibition*, Fondazione La Biennale di Venezia, 2011

Baron van Dedem, Willem, and D. Aronson, *The European Fine Art Fair Maastricht*, The European Fine Art Foundation, 2006–15

Bethenod, Martin, *FIAC*, Foire Internationale d'Art Contemporain, Paris, 2005–15

Cortes Munoz, L.E., *ARCO*, Madrid, 2011

Martin, J., *Art Dubai*, Dubai, 2008

McAndrew, Clare, *The International Art Market Reports*, The European
    Fine Art Foundation, 2010–15

Misa Shin, *Art Fair Tokyo*, 2007

Stomiene, D., *Art Vilnius*, Vilnius, 2009

Sykes, S., *DIFC Gulf Art Fair*, Dubai International Financial Centre, 2007

THE IMPACT OF NEW TECHNOLOGY ON ART

The rise of information and communication technologies (ICT), regarded as the third Industrial Revolution, has caused great economic, technological and sociocultural change today. Information technologies are omnipresent in modern life, fuelling the digital economy while accelerating the production, distribution and consumption of goods and services. New technologies have left no field untouched, and the arts are no exception. Information and communication technologies have accelerated consumption in art markets, as the internet facilitates global operations and new business models reinforce or complement the established art ecosystem. Art institutions increasingly embrace new media for the display, promotion and conservation of their collections, aiming to create a unique experience for their visitors. Artists engage with social media as cultural branding intensifies in the digital age, while experimenting with new media gives rise to new art forms that push the boundaries of contemporary art and museum collections.

In other industries, digital technologies have empowered entrepreneurs to create new business models directly linking producers and consumers while bypassing gatekeepers and intermediaries. According to Clare McAndrew, the art world has proven more reluctant to transform based on the dynamics of e-business. This is because the construction of what Pierre Bourdieu (1930–2002) refers to as 'symbolic value' – the perceived significance of a work of art in the minds of art professionals and the audience – depends largely on the physical presence of established intermediaries in the art market. However this condition has started to change recently as art entrepreneurs and traditional art businesses now view digital technologies as an opportunity to reach new markets and deliver more value to their clients and audience. In the digital age, the art business and technology are fundamentally entangled. Technologies facilitate operations and collaborations in the art world, and art businesses provide fertile ground for the development and application of technologies. In other words, technologies, business and culture converge in order to promote art and provide richer experiences for buyers and audiences.

International contemporary art, especially since 1989, prospers in a rapidly changing, neoliberal and global environment. Internet technologies, in particular, have triggered instant communication and information delivery, connecting users across the globe, affecting the organisation of art production and consumption. Artistic production and consumption are no longer limited to cities and this globalisation has in turn altered the relationship between artists, buyers, audiences and the place of artistic production. Artists are able to expose their work worldwide and gain access to markets that were impossible to reach before. Newly emerging art markets such as Brazil, India, West and South Africa or South East Asia have gained momentum and exposure because those markets are now interconnected with the core art hubs of London, Paris and New York. In a more subtle way new technologies have increased transparency in terms of prices of works of art, especially auction prices, and in this way collectors can take more informed decisions regarding art investments. In general, auction houses, such as Sotheby's or Christie's, and auction platforms like Auctionata facilitate online sales in which values paid are accessible by the public online. The fact that more information about art works' prices is available online has intensified the view of art as investment which is based on actual evidence and not only intuition. Nevertheless, online platforms do not always guarantee full transparency of prices, as in a few cases the online channel is preferred by buyers who do not want to expose their identity in a physical sale.

Information technologies have intensified the globalisation of art, as local galleries are able to sell the work of local artists abroad and galleries from emerging economies are able to connect the work of local artists with foreign collectors. Immediacy in communications accelerates the creation of a global contemporary art market that integrates many local art markets in the form of a single, unified and interconnected field of contemporary art that transcends urban and national boundaries. As a result, contemporary art develops in two tiers: as local avant-gardes at the fringes of the many art sectors, and as a global commodity disseminated instantly across institutional and national boundaries.

In addition, information technologies have fuelled entrepreneurship in the artistic field, empowering agents to create value in the art market through the development of online business models. According to McAndrew, the online art market ecology has evolved in three stages. The first coincided with the early dissemination of internet technologies in the mid-1990s, as a few online galleries, such as art.com, emerged selling their own stock online. During the second stage that started in the mid-2000s, existing players, such as Sotheby's and Christie's, Saatchi Gallery and Gagosian Gallery acquired an online presence. The third stage occurred after 2010, as the online art market ecology has been enriched with the entry of intermediaries such as Artsy, Saatchi Online (now Saatchi Art) and Etsy, all of which sell the stock of third parties. Interestingly, an increasing number of online art businesses target niche markets. ArtViatic, for example, facilitates collector-to-collector trading. At the same time, online auction platforms such as Artnet, Auctionata and Paddle8 are gaining momentum. Online art entrepreneurs create value through digital networks that bypass intermediaries, linking producers directly to consumers, a process which is known as disintermediation. Nowadays, these entrepreneurs attempt to create value at different parts of the art ecosystem. Online art businesses have lower information and transaction costs, linking supply and demand for art efficiently. Nevertheless, they do not replace traditional art businesses or the role of the dealer, which are still vital in introducing new artists to the market and managing artists' reputations in the art world. While the high-end sectors of the art market are mainly served by major-league auction houses and art galleries, online art business has sustained the low and middle segments of the market, as almost 90 per cent of art traded online sells for up to $50,000.

According to the TEFAF Market Report 2015, 6 per cent of online art sales are over $500,000 with only 1 per cent of unit prices over a million dollars. For some, high-end online transactions are attractive as they offer anonymity, but the majority of blue-chip art collectors appreciate the glamorous experience of participating at live auction. The online art business is, therefore, not expected to perform in a similar way to online retail in general, such as Amazon or eBay, both of which create value for the customer by offering a wider selection of products at lower prices. The consumption of art, especially at the top end of the market, is a luxury experience, which is provided by prestigious brands in the art market. In comparison with online retailers, which compete on the basis of price, selection and service for customers, art businesses – both online and physical – rely on creating value for artists through their personal relationships and professional networks. This is because the process of value creation derives from the cultural perception of the business, which is based on the recognition of art world professionals as connoisseurs of the works they deal in. As a result, established galleries, art foundations and auction houses maintain their advantage over the online world, capitalising on the trust made tangible by their physical presence. Online art businesses exploit the low and middle segments of the market by exposing a wider range of artists. Their competitive advantage relies on allowing users to 'discover' new art based on algorithms that track their past behaviour and preferences. In other words, their business models perform based on the long tail effect as online galleries, free from the constraints of a physical space, are able to expose a wider selection of emerging artists to critical and commercial appreciation. Saatchi Art, for instance, applies a free access policy to all artists (taking 30 per cent commission on sales), and thus users can discover a huge number of artists across the globe. Artspace Auctions, which is an online marketplace specialising in contemporary art, takes no commission from sellers, as buyers pay premium equal to 15 per cent of the successful bid price.

Online art galleries may reduce inequalities in the art market by democratising access to artists. However, recently online art businesses have emerged with the support of powerful agents from the art and business worlds. The example of Artsy, which is an aggregator of art market information and an online trading platform, is a typical case of a new venture that seeks to dominate the online art market. Cornering the support of entrepreneurs and celebrities, Artsy managed to raise an initial capital of $5.4 million. Although it is believed that information and communication technologies could decentralise the power structure of the art world, offering the possibility of independence from the established art market, initiatives like Artsy show that large-scale investments can concentrate both centres of activities and power into a single platform. These new interdependencies are increasingly common as the worlds of art and business converge, and agents from the art world seek partnerships in the business sphere. The recent collaboration between Sotheby's and eBay launches the beginning of a new era in which traditional firms within the art world partner with technological companies and online platforms in order to create new audiences. Competition is intensified as more players from technology initiate operations within the art world, such as Amazon Art, which is an online marketplace that sells original and limited-edition fine art from selected galleries.

The convergence between art and commerce changes the art world which transforms in tandem with technology and business, leading to interdependencies between all three disciplines. A recent partnership between the crowdfunding platform Kickstarter and Art Basel aims to support innovative art. Interestingly, in this case the crowd, and not art dealers or curators, decides and distinguishes which projects will be realised, thereby democratising artistic production. Ultimately, new technologies enrich the art market ecosystem, providing significant support to the margins by exposing and supporting artists and projects that do not otherwise have access to the art world.

Information and communication technologies have also gained momentum within art institutions which incorporate digital technologies to enrich audience experience in terms of on-site and online learning. Firstly, digital technologies enhance the museum experience for visitors as providers of information about the exhibits, which are often interactive. Apart from audio aids, enhanced media guides, interactive labels, mobile applications and augmented reality applications are now used in the museum context, and curators are increasingly factoring these technologies into their exhibition planning. Enhanced media guides provide a tour of an exhibition, often including a narrative developed by the curator and multimedia. Similarly, QR codes are used in art galleries and museums, enabling users to retrieve information about the work by scanning a graphic code similar to a barcode. In the Museum of New Art in Tasmania, Australia, wireless sensors detect the location and movement of visitors, providing information on smart devices about nearby art works. Mobile applications invite visitors to use their smartphones to retrieve information, and in some cases to co-create the work of art in augmented reality space.

The emergence and dissemination of smart devices have fuelled mobile applications, which in turn have an impact on the art world. Mobile apps enable the organisers of art fairs to assist visitors to navigate the fair and the city by providing live location-based information that connects users, exhibits and events. These applications are also designed to discover and experience art beyond art institutions. Street Art London is a mobile app that ushers users through the urban space of London in order to uncover street art. The Google Art Project is an example of an interdisciplinary collaboration between the high-technology firm and museums around the world in order to create virtual tours within their collections. Virtual tours promote museums' collections and permit access from a distance, enabling art professionals and the broader audience to 'virtually visit' museums around the world. This customised learning experience for visitors applied by galleries, museums and fairs marks a paradigm shift to a customised service that meets the needs and expectations of individual visitors, rather than a standardised service for a broad market. The increased use of online resources from users generates useful personal information. Marketing analytics nowadays, fuelled by the power of big data, enhance the understanding of audience behaviour before, during and after a visit, and this information feeds into the institution's programming patterns, their retail activities and the ways in which they engage with online and offline communities. Importantly, digital resources are a crucial tool in the hands of museums, galleries and archive resources to fulfil their educational remit.

In addition, information technologies also contribute to conservational issues, while in some cases 3D printing helps to recreate damaged art objects. The role of technologies with regards to conservation can be broader including the use of X-radiography, which can reveal useful information about the condition and construction of an art work, as well as compositional changes and hidden images not visible to the naked eye. By using X-rays scientists have discovered that Leonardo da Vinci created the *Mona Lisa* using a technique known as *smufato*, mixing thin layers of pigment, glaze and oil in order to depict shadows in an incredibly realistic way.

New media, and specifically social media, have contributed to the dissemination of art. Artists like Ai Weiwei (b.1958) use social media, such as social networks and blogs in order to promote their activities, to interact with their fan base and construct their identities online. Social media are an essential component of cultural branding, as artists construct authenticity in the form of digital narratives that increase visibility and emotional engagement with the audience. Artists also appropriate digital technologies in artistic creativity as a tool, for example creating photomontages. As a medium, technology can be used for the creation of new art forms, such as the invention of the video camera leading to video art, or digital design leading to new art such as digital sculpture. Digital technologies used as a 'medium' of artistic practice have a long history that derives from the invention of computers and their appropriation in the 1960s in the first exhibitions on art and technology. *Cybernetic Serendipity* (1968, London), *Les Immatériaux* (1985, Paris), *Data Dynamics* (2001, New York), *Incheon Digital Art Festival* (Incheon, 2010) and *Electronic Superhighway: 2016–1966* (2016, London) all exhibitions that explore interdisciplinary intersections between art and technology.

As radical experiments in art and technologies, these works of art are installations that experiment with software and space, aiming to engage the audience in an interactive experience. As the technological medium progresses and as more artists incorporate digital technologies within their artistic practices, we are also seeing the creation of database art, internet art, satellite art or big data art. The tension between fine art and new media art is unresolved, as the latter is occasionally considered 'science' instead of art, and partially a niche of contemporary art. Ars Electronica in Linz, La Gaîté Lyrique in Paris and the Foundation for Art and Creative Technologies (FACT) in Liverpool are alternative institutional structures devoted to interdisciplinary art, supporting avant-garde projects that explore the intersection of art and technology.

Although new technologies represent a liberating dynamic that should reduce inequalities in the artistic field, new points of power concentration, such as the online intermediaries Artsy and Saatchi Art, are expected to emerge receiving the support of business, technological and cultural elites. According to Henry Jenkins, media convergence is fuelled by collective intelligence as a driver for sociocultural, economic and technological changes. In the artistic field collective intelligence influences the production and consumption of art in terms of crowdfunding and democratisation of selection; in terms of art institutions which develop services based on visitor-generated data; in terms of online art galleries that allow users' behaviour and preferences to shape trends and popularity of artists; in terms of mobile applications through which users upload and share information about art works, exhibitions and urban experiences; and lastly, in terms of art critiques which take place as users interact on social media.

Reflecting the transformation of the global economy and the growth of ultra-high net worth individuals in emerging economies, information and communication technologies accelerate the dissemination and consumption of art around the globe. Progressively new technologies have led to a paradigm shift in the production and consumption of art, giving rise to novel structures for art business, which are supported by the new interdependencies between art, technology and commerce.

Marios Samdanis

Bibliography

Adam, Georgina, *Big Bucks: The Explosion of the Art Market in the 21st Century*, Lund Humphries, 2014

Anderson, Chris, 'The Long Tail', *Wired Magazine Archive*, http://archive.wired.com/wired/archive/12.10/tail.html

George, Adrian, *The Curator's Handbook: Museums, Commercial Galleries, Independent Spaces*, Thames & Hudson, 2015

Jenkins, Henry, 'The Cultural Logic of Media Convergence', *International Journal of Cultural Studies*, vol.7, issue 1, 2004, pp 33–43

Khaire, Mukti, 'Art without borders? Online Firms and the Global Art Market', in Velthuis, Olav, and Stefano B. Curioni, (eds), *Cosmopolitan Canvases: The Globalization of Markets for Contemporary Art*, Oxford University Press, 2015

McAndrew, Clare, *TEFAF Maastricht Art Market Report 2015*, European Fine Art Foundation, 2015

Paul, Christiane, *Digital Art*, Thames & Hudson, 2003

Preece, Chloe, 'The Authentic Celebrity Brand: Unpacking Ai Weiwei's Celebritised Selves', *Journal of Marketing Management*, vol.31, nos 5–6, 2015, pp 616–45

Velthuis, Olav, and Stefano B. Curioni, 'Making Markets Global', in Velthuis, Olav, and Stefano B. Curioni, (eds), *Cosmopolitan Canvases: The Globalization of Markets for Contemporary Art*, Oxford University Press, 2015

Zoran, Amit, and Leah Buechley, 'Hybrid Reassemblage: An Exploration of Craft, Digital Fabrication and Artifact Uniqueness', *Leonardo*, vol.46, no.1, 2013, pp 4–10

DEALERS AND COLLECTORS

ARTIST–DEALER RELATIONSHIPS

Critical to the understanding of the structure of the art world is an appreciation of the importance of networks, namely complex sets of social and economic relationships, which can include cooperation and competition. Economic action is embedded in structures of social relations rather than being decided largely on the basis of a calculation of costs and benefits. It is not surprising that social relationships are important: art is aesthetic essentially non-utilitarian and with psychic or non-monetary benefit.

The artist-dealer relationship has been described as a joint venture or protracted partnership. This description, in a discussion of contracts between the arts and commerce, assumes a living artist and a dealer having a bilateral financial agreement in order to provide an income to both artist and dealer. It refers to primary market art sales where works of art are sold for the first time with the dealer facilitating the sale including the negotiation of the sale price with the buyer. What is the nature of the artist–dealer relationship? Moreover, why does the artist–dealer relationship as a joint venture partnership continue in a market economy increasingly marked by digital platforms? Why is there so little direct selling by artists? In other words, what is the value of the dealer, an intermediary, to the artist to warrant a conventional commission of 50 per cent of the sales price of each art work sold by the dealer?

The dealer representing artists in primary art market sales may prefer the term gallerist, which is a desire to present a less overtly commercial gloss to the joint venture partnership, as dealing connotes transactional seller–buyer commercial exchanges. The term gallerist suggests a gallery space used to exhibit the works of represented artists with the general public invited to visit as spectators (so making a distinction between both private dealers of contemporary art operating without exhibition space available to the general public and secondary market dealers who do not represent living artists). In this regard, Marcel Duchamp (1887–1968) recognised the importance of audience reception, principally that the artist relies on an audience to complete the work. The spectator is considered the starting point of the work (if it is to assume any social value), as Duchamp includes the possibility of posterity in the primers of art history. The dealer's value to the artist is to provide access to an audience of spectators, an elastic term including art appreciators, critics, curators and collectors (representing both private individuals and institutions). This access includes the exhibition space of the dealer and the presentation of the artist at art fairs; in addition, reputation management of the artist includes communications with curators and critics. The successful dealer is deemed to understand the business of the art world, which includes social relations to mediate complex exchanges between artists and buyers (i.e. spectators with the economic means and inclination to buy works of art). Following additional purchases of art, some of these buyers may be treated by dealers as collectors – an elite buyer category. By securing the works of represented artists in prominent art museums, ideally in the form of bequests by collectors, art can be an important start to posterity (for the work of art and the collector, who is acknowledged alongside the work). Posterity includes the writing of contemporary art history, usually relying on publicly available works.

The ascendancy of contemporary art during the last three decades, which includes the appearance of contemporary art being resold at auction, is also marked by the rise of larger dealers with the top 20 operating multiple exhibition spaces often in two or more countries. There has also been greater diversity in the contemporary sector: more women as dealers of contemporary art; greater gender balance of artists represented by contemporary art dealers; the rise of non-Western artists being represented by the largest dealers; and the profile of contemporary art collectors becoming more international, reflecting patterns of economic development and distribution of private wealth. In a market sector noted for low levels of regulation, art consultants and art advisers have also been attracted by rising prices for contemporary art as new intermediaries in art transactions between the dealer and the buyer.

Division of labour underpins the artist–dealer relationship as a joint venture partnership, which is to say that artists and dealers have different expertise and skills. Contemporary art dealers usually maintain owner-operated businesses (as often indicated by the names of galleries, such as Gagosian Gallery, Marian Goodman Gallery, Hauser & Wirth, Sprüth Magers, Sadie Coles HQ and Victoria Miro). The successful dealer of contemporary art is deemed to possess good aesthetic judgement in identifying and developing artistic talent. In addition, the successful dealer needs to cultivate a network of collectors to support the financial side of the business. This includes fostering trust and confidence in the taste of the dealer as an arbiter of contemporary art in recognition that the reputations of artists are in the process of being shaped. It is telling that larger dealerships, those representing more than 30 artists, may start to adopt bureaucratic structures such as adopting specialist staff for sales and artist representation, even if the owner-operator dealer reserves the right to make decisions on which artists are represented and final sale prices. A dealer who prefers to use the term gallerist, as indicated above, may wish to accentuate the aesthetic side of representing artists. When dealing both with artists and collectors, subjective and relational factors matter such that the lifecycle of the dealer's business – including the name of the gallery – is usually limited to the working life of the dealer. For example, when Anthony d'Offay (b.1940) retired from active dealing he closed his eponymous gallery in London with artists migrating to other dealers. The gallery run by Leo Castelli (1907–99) operates under the management of his third wife by re-emphasising his legacy in the development of Pop, minimal and conceptual art.

Representation is key to the artist–dealer relationship. It is a commercial relationship and yet, at the same time, there is a high investment of labour (measured in time, social commitment and emotions) to ensure that the relationship continues. The dealer's role in representing the artist includes exhibiting the artist's works in the dealer's gallery space, promoting the artist to curators and critics for favourable reviews so that the artist may be exhibited in public art institutions, and facilitating sales of the artist's works to private collectors and institutions (such as art museums, foundations and business corporations). Ideally, a dealer aims to manage the sale prices of represented artists with rising reputations to avoid speculative flipping (a tendency associated with any asset subject to quick price appreciation). A critical part of reputation management, for both the artist and dealer, is the placing of a work of art with a so-called trusted buyer rather than selling to the highest bidder (as there is no legal obligation to offer resales back to the dealer). A dealer may represent a handful of artists or several dozen; from a commercial perspective it is an issue of diversification or portfolio management as it is risky to rely on just one or two artists. Aesthetic choices behind selecting each artist include how the artists sit alongside each other as part of the gallerist's own practice. Represented artists, who help to articulate a gallerist's aesthetic practice, provide signals to the art market regarding the dealer's stature relative to other dealers and peers. Relative bargaining power, particularly in the absence of contracts, usually favours the dealer. If the artist is represented solely by the dealer, this may include an exclusive distribution relationship. In addition, representation by a dealer includes a condition that the artist does not engage in direct selling. The dealer's justification is the value that they add to the art of the artist and this is often reflected in the negotiated sale price paid by a buyer.

The successful fostering and maintenance of this relationship is therefore essential. Disharmonious relationships between artists and dealers occur with several typical scenarios that may lead to separation. Firstly, an artist could feel neglected by the dealer, which can occur in the largest dealerships representing 50–100 artists. Secondly, a change in the artist's practice could run counter to the dealer's taste or what the dealer feels is commercially attractive to the market. Furthermore, the reputation of the artist will often start to outstrip the reputation of the dealer, and the artist would then be more attractive to more prominent and larger dealers.

Entrepreneurial activity disrupting the conventional artist–dealer relationship does not occur so frequently, although at the high end of the market Damien Hirst could be cited as an example of this. His *Beautiful Inside My Head Forever* sale of works by auction at Sotheby's, London on 15–16 September 2008 (memorable as it coincided with the financial collapse of Lehman Brothers) raised $146 million in 223 lots. Hirst had sufficient superstar status and bargaining power to bypass his dealers and to negotiate a favourable consignor's commission with Sotheby's. At the lower end of the market, Saatchi Online was established in 2006 by leading collector of contemporary art Charles Saatchi to represent lesser-known artists and to sell works for modest prices. Now operating as Saatchi Art without the eponymous collector's involvement it and remains a platform to match artists with buyers, with artists receiving 70 per cent of the sale price.

Why has representation of artists not followed, say, the management agency model used in popular entertainment or professional sports? This question draws on Sherwin Rosen's 'economics of superstars' thesis, based on the concentration of rewards among a few talented top performers in particular industrial sectors. In 2015 United Talent Agency (UTA), a new Hollywood-based agency competing against Creative Artists Agency (CAA), launched UTA Fine Arts. The crossover potential from the fine arts to the popular arts is high as particular artists are eager to branch out into, for example, fashion, music or film. However, UTA Fine Arts does not sell art but plans to work in partnership with existing dealers who represent artists on projects that may attract wider popular and commercial appeal. The current art market ecosystem of the dealer as an intermediary between producer (artist) and consumer (collector) is supported by both artists and collectors. In this regard UTA Fine Arts may be viewed as an additional intermediary, operating on a commission basis, offering skills and contacts to help artists pursue new crossover projects and negotiate contracts.

The successful dealer is good at the core aspects of intermediation between artists and audiences. Getting the artist exhibited is important. Artists like spectators, even those who are not collectors. The dealer's role in adding value for the artist may also be reflected in the sale prices paid by the right, trusted collectors (unmotivated by the short-term financial gain of reselling the work). Collectors of contemporary art are also buying into the aesthetic tastes of preferred dealers who see themselves as important gate-keepers, and any activities that do not add value for either artist or collector have to be pared down or eliminated. Of course 'value' is an elastic term that means different things to artists and collectors. An artist may value being loved by a dealer, which is labour-intensive and challenging to maintain if the dealer is representing many artists. A collector may wish to collect new artists, which represents risk investment by the dealer for uncertain returns. Any failure to reconcile the needs and ambitions of artists and collectors runs the commercial liability of not maintaining a viable business operation.

Derrick Chong

Bibliography

Baudrillard, Jean, 'The System of Collecting', trans. by R. Cardinal in J. Elsner and
    R. Cardinal (eds), *Cultures of Collecting*, Reaktion Books, 1994, pp 7–24

Belk, Russell, et al., 'Collectors and Collecting', *Advances in Consumer Research*,
    no.15, 1998, pp 548–53

Caves, Richard, 'Contracts between Art and Commerce', *Journal of Economic
    Perspectives*, vol.2, no.17, 2003, pp 73–84

Duchamp, Marcel, 'The Creative Act', in M. Sansouillet and E. Peterson (eds),
    The Essential Writings of Marcel Duchamp, Thames and Hudson, 1975,
    pp 138–40

Duncan, Carol, *Civilizing Rituals: Inside Public Art Museums*, Routledge, 1995

Granovetter, Mark, 'Economic Action and Social Structure: The Problem of
    Embeddedness', *American Journal of Sociology*, vol.91, issue 3, 1985, pp 481–510

Rosen, Sherwin, 'The Economics of Superstars', *American Economic Review*,
    vol.71, issue 5, December 1981, pp 845–58

Steyerl, Hito, 'Is the Museum a Battlefield?', performance-lecture, 13th Istanbul
    Biennal, Stedelijk Museum, 2012

COLLECTOR–DEALER RELATIONSHIPS

The complexity of trust and the social relationship that dealers have to build up with their artists are equally important in dealings with collectors. Art is thinly traded in an environment that is marked by low regulation; moreover, contemporary art has the additional market characteristics of unlimited supply and greater opportunities for key players to shape taste. Most players – dealers and auction houses as the key intermediaries – are privately held firms (with Sotheby's as a notable exception trading on the New York Stock Exchange as BID) so do not report annual totals for revenues or profits as part of audited financial statements released to the public, and any amounts reported may not be verifiable.

The collector–dealer relationship needs to benefit both parties. Cultivating ongoing exchanges beyond the one-off economic transaction seem to describe the relationship. As part of greater research into the workings of the art market and art business organisations in various areas, recent attention has turned to economic sociology, which applies sociological tools and concepts to gain a deeper understanding of organisations and the economy. One particular concept in economic sociology is embeddedness, associated with Mark Granovetter, as a way to capture the idea that the actions of actors are importantly refracted by the social relations within which they function. Though Granovetter was not addressing the art market, actors can refer to collectors and dealers and the social relations that resonate within the art scene and the art market. The preference for social relations is a necessary condition for trust and trustworthy behaviour. Concrete personal relations and structures of such relations generate trust and discourage malfeasance, although there is equal opportunity for conflict in these scenarios. For example, there have been periodic cases of so-called confidence rackets or embezzlement involving art market professionals as reported in *The Art*

Newspaper. Primary market dealers will wish to have some control over the resales of artists they represent. This may involve competitive pricing (such as speculative buying to resell), which is negatively sanctioned even though this would be profitable for individual collectors.

To appreciate the collector–dealer relationship is to understand the nature of collectors and collecting. The collector often relies on an intermediary to secure works of art. Collecting art is, from a historical perspective, an elite recreational activity. Possessions are a form of self-definition with the visible nature of art projecting the collector's judgement and taste. Moreover, the self-enhancing motives of power, prestige, control and mastery may underpin why art is collected. Collecting is an intensely involving form of consumption (as distinct from accumulation and hoarding) and seldom begins purposefully; rather one is revealed (or discovered) to be a collector over time. French philosopher Jean Baudrillard (1929–2007) has discussed the role of absence, such that the collector is marked by the simultaneous desire and fear of completing a collection. The dealer may play a role in fostering the compulsive aspects that pervade collecting. That collections tend toward specialisation means that collectors may develop relationships with particular dealers and are likely to make repeat purchases over a period of time. The role of the dealer certainly helps to legitimise the acquisition of art as collecting. There is a conversion of the object from the profane (commodity exchange in making the acquisition) to the sacred when it becomes part of something deemed by the collector to be a collection. A self-referential system of collector and collection exists and this is not surprising as collections serve as extensions of the collector's self.

Given the intermediary role of the dealer there are several challenges to the collector–dealer relationship. Firstly, new intermediaries can disrupt the relationship by creating different relationships that are valued by the collector, such as the rise of art advisers (or art consultants) and interior designers as new intermediaries between dealer and collector. This can erode the conventional and direct-access relationship between the dealer and the collector, particularly if the collector trusts the adviser/consultant to make purchases. This also confers bargaining power on the largest advisers/consultants. The second challenge relates to auction houses who are able to change their conventional business model of arranging auctions, which can pose a challenge to dealers as interdependent firms – with separate and complementary roles – in the art market. This includes private treaty sales by auction houses (operating like dealers) or auction houses buying dealerships (such as Sotheby's purchase of Noortman Master Painting and Christie's purchase of Haunch of Venison). (The limited lifespan of auction house hook-ups with dealers may suggest the fate of Sotheby's recent purchase of art adviser service Art Agency, Partners.) Thirdly, the financialisation of art as a product, instead of a passion investment or emotional asset, complicates how art is promoted by dealers. What is the benefit or value of owning a work of art? Is art an investment good or a consumption good? If art is seen as an investment, the assumption is that a return is desired on that investment, in turn challenging the dominant discourse of aesthetic judgements. However, analysis of the business of art collection recognises the intersection of globalisation and high net worth wealth, as reflected in the annual World Wealth Report (published by Capgemini and RBC Wealth Management), that invites both the homogenisation of taste and the pluralisation of consumption in modern and contemporary art. This means new buyers of contemporary art may wish to realise capital appreciation within several years by reselling works at auction (as opposed to reoffering the work to the dealer). It also means that some sectors of the art market may be challenged to attract new buyers if capital appreciation is less likely to occur.

The public art museum is a key feature in collector–dealer relations. Collectors of art fall into two main categories: institutions such as public art museums and private art foundations or museums; and business corporations and private individuals. Of course, some private collectors, such as those cited by *ARTnews* in its annual review, behave like institutional collectors, such as by creating private art museums or art foundations. (See 'Private Museums'.) Patrons of art have made an important contribution to the history of civilisation. The formation of public art museum collections, in the US and Europe, has relied on the beneficence of individual art collectors. It is likely that the taste of private collectors will continue to inform the permanent collections of public institutions. However, we are also witnessing the growth of private museum projects by leading collectors of contemporary art (such as Boros in Berlin, Pinault in Venice, Rubell in Miami, Saatchi in London, and many more initiatives of private museums of contemporary art from Asia). Favourable taxation is certainly a factor in the US with the Internal Revenue Service (IRS) interested in the operations of the new private art museums. Whether these initiatives will survive the death of the founder-collector – in the tradition of Peggy Guggenheim (Venice), Isabella Stewart Gardner (Boston), Henry Clay Frick (New York), and the first four Marquesses of Hertford and Sir Richard Wallace, son of the 4th Marquess (London) – is too early to determine.

The goal of art is to find a home; indeed, provenance, as a term used to denote ownership history of the work since it was created, is deemed valuable. Post-mortem distribution problems are significant to collectors and their families (as keeping one's collection intact may be a way to gain a sort of immortality). The most valued repository of art is the public art museum as it enhances both the cultural value (some art works enter art history texts) and potentially the economic value of the objects therein. With this in mind, the significance of the term 'museum quality' is better appreciated: it is used as sales patter by dealers and auctioneers to signal works of the highest aesthetic value – that is to say, worthy to be on display in a public art museum. In some cases, a dealer, cataloguer or auctioneer will reference a comparable work in a public collection for the purposes of indicating comparative value, with aesthetic or intrinsic value being translated into an economic price. A related promotional tactic of dealers is to include NFS (not for sale) works in exhibitions – not unlike works that are featured in public art museums – to create an aura of desire geared to appeal to private collectors. This is somewhat ironic as the formation of the public art museum is cited as an example of a democratising institution, as distinct from private collections associated with royalty; for example the establishment of the Louvre in the aftermath of the French Revolution. Indeed, as Berlin-based filmmaker and artist Hito Steyerl (b.1966) reminds us in her performance-lecture *Is the Museum a Battlefield?*, the history of art museums – such as the Louvre's change of use from royal palace to public art museum – is the result of revolutions.

Arguably dealers prefer to place works with private collectors who have expressed intentions of donating works to public collections. In the primary market sale the dealer may not need to discount the selling price for a private collector beyond 10 to 15 per cent (whereas a museum may require a more substantial cut of 25 to 40 per cent). In an ideal scenario, the work is donated to a major museum, as opposed to being resold on the secondary market, which also enhances the reputations of both artist and dealer.

Derrick Chong

Bibliography

Baudrillard, Jean, 'The System of Collecting', trans. by R. Cardinal in J. Elsner
    and R. Cardinal (eds), *Cultures of Collecting*, Reaktion Books, 1994, pp 7–24
Belk, Russell, et al., 'Collectors and Collecting', *Advances in Consumer Research*,
    no.15, 1998, pp 548–53
Caves, Richard, 'Contracts between Art and Commerce', *Journal of Economic
    Perspectives*, vol.2, no.17, 2003, pp 73–84
Duchamp, Marcel, 'The Creative Act', in M. Sansouillet and E. Peterson (eds),
    The Essential Writings of Marcel Duchamp, Thames and Hudson, 1975,
    pp 138–40
Duncan, Carol, *Civilizing Rituals: Inside Public Art Museums*, Routledge, 1995
Granovetter, Mark, 'Economic Action and Social Structure: The Problem of
    Embeddedness', *American Journal of Sociology*, vol.91, issue 3, 1985, pp 481–510
Rosen, Sherwin, 'The Economics of Superstars', *American Economic Review*,
    vol.71, issue 5, December 1981, pp 845–58
Steyerl, Hito, 'Is the Museum a Battlefield?', performance-lecture, 13th Istanbul
    Biennal, Stedelijk Museum, 2012

ART AS INVESTMENT

With over a fifth of high net worth individuals' (HNWI) wealth channelled into art, the global art investment fund market is worth well over $1 billion today. The consensus amongst private banks and managers is that art and collectibles should be included in traditional wealth management. The notion of art as an investment is as old as art itself. If art is portable then it is a security. The value of art as a fixed asset is less certain, because it is something that we should be able to barter for something that we might need. In times of war, famine or other natural or manmade disasters it can be exchanged for food and water, albeit at a fraction of its value under normal economic conditions. In this sense it is an investment in life itself. The crucial factor is not, as one might suppose, the economic returns that art may generate over time, although in recent years this has become a fixation of investors and the art market, but its liquidity. A work of art only has value or use if it can be exchanged for something else that we need at the time.

Art, famously, does not produce a fiscal dividend for its investor, although some have argued that it does afford a non-pecuniary reward. It is, like gold and diamonds, sterile because it does not earn money for its owner in the form of interest. The value of the reward is measured according to the amount of time the owner devotes to the appreciation of their possession. David Rockefeller (b.1915) is reputed to have enjoyed solitary twilight strolls through his collection, caressing his marble statues and imbibing the beauty of his paintings. Non-pecuniary benefit is more commonly experienced with other arts, particularly music, which requires no more than the investment of one's time. One of the world's most successful art dealers, Joseph Duveen (1869–1939), didn't believe that art was a commodity at all, to be bought as you would copper or tin. Great paintings, he asserted, were immune to the performance of the stock market. This view is apparent today in the acquisition of art trophies for exorbitant prices in spite, or perhaps because, of uncertain economic conditions. And yet art has become integrated into the financial system. International contemporary art is now valued for its liquidity and accelerated financial growth, which is why financial vehicles have been devised to accommodate investor sentiment. The type of fiscal instruments that have been thought up for art mirror those for other commodities, in particular passion goods: precious metals, wine and jewels. The favourite structure is the private equity fund, registered offshore and not subject to Financial Service Authority regulation.

The Fine Art Fund is a private closed-equity financial instrument active across a number of sectors of the fine art category from Old Masters to international contemporary art, as well as sub-sectors such as photography. The fund, which was established in 2005 at the beginning of the greatest ever surge in art prices, atypically offers its investors the loan of the pictures in its possession, in lieu of a financial dividend. Lending art is perhaps the only way in which an investor might secure a fee, but the incentive to this behaviour is capital gains and tax efficiency. A judicious donation of a significant work of art by a private owner to a public or publicly accessible museum in the UK offers a means of offsetting the fiscal tax burden. It also adds credibility to the work of art, expressed as validation in the market for contemporary art and authentication in the case of the art of the past. A wholesale example of this practice is probably the English country house. The owners under a private trust (such as Chatsworth) or acceptance in lieu scheme (such as Houghton) are able to continue to derive enjoyment or non-pecuniary benefit from their collection, which remains in situ. Francis Ronald Egerton, 7th Duke of Sutherland (b.1940), whose ancestors acquired innumerable masterpieces for the Bridgewater Estate at the art sales of the Duc d'Orléans at the end of the eighteenth century, successfully sold two of the six *poesie* paintings by Titian (*c.*1485/90–1576) which were on long-term loan to the National Gallery of Scotland, for a total of $147.25 million. It is highly unlikely that the coal merchant Francis Egerton, 3rd Duke of Bridgewater, considered his acquisition in 1798 a base investment, but the capital returns for his distant descendant were, nevertheless, huge. The 3rd Duke of Bridgewater paid £2,625 for each work (today £346,543). The current market value for *Diana and Actaeon* (1558) was estimated to be twice the $77.5 million paid for it by the National Gallery in London and the National Gallery of Scotland. Another work in the series, *Diana and Callisto* (1556–9) was acquired for the nation by the same two museums for $69.75 million. Both prices reflect the unprecedented rise in value over the last 25 years of works of exceptional quality, rarity and national significance. In 1972 the National Gallery acquired another work in the series, *The Death of Actaeon* (1559–75), for a mere £1.8 million (today £17.3 million). *Perseus and Andromeda* (1554–56), another work in Titian's *poesie* series, now a part of the Wallace Collection by inheritance, was acquired at auction for £326 10s (today £43,037) in 1815 by the Marquess of Hertford. Yet another picture in the set, *The Rape of Europa* (1560–2), proved rather more liquid. It sold to Lord Berwick for £735 (today £97,032) in the 1798 sale; it sold again 12 years later for £309 15s (today £27,496) and again for £288 10s (today £39,245) in 1852 to the Earl of Darnley, until finally coming to rest in Boston in 1896 for the princely sum of £20,500 (today £2.9 million) in the collection of Isabella Stewart Gardner.

The volatility of the traditionally stable Old Master painting market in the second decade of the twenty-first century is highlighted by the fluctuating fortunes of another painting, *Portrait of a Man, Half-Length, with Arms Akimbo* (1658) by Rembrandt (1606–69). The painting, thought by expert Jan van der Wetering to have been cut at the base, sold at Christie's in London for $31 million in 2009. Its market price in 2012, according to its current owner, New York art dealer Otto Naumann, is $47 million, who established to his satisfaction that the work was not in fact cut. The work was originally sold by an English gentleman in 1930 for £18,500 (today £1 million). The great hike in Old Master prices, although receiving a boost in the 1930s from the bravura of Joseph Duveen, was truly ignited in the late 1980s and early 1990s. Duveen was a price-setter as much as a market maker. He noticed in the first decades of the twentieth century, and deep into the recession of the 1930s, that significant numbers of American industrialists had a great deal of cash and financially embarrassed European aristocrats had a lot of great art. He simply brought the two parties together and conjured a value. American buying of European and international contemporary and modern art continues to this day. The Getty Museum acquired a bronze *Dancing Faun* (1610–15) by the Baroque sculptor Adriaen de Vries

(1550–1626) for £10.88 million in 1989, a price that fell within the estimate. A second, slightly larger, de Vries sculpture, *Mythological Figure Holding a Globe* (1626), broke all records for the artist when it was sold through Christie's to the Rijksmuseum in Amsterdam for $27.8 million in 2014. The main Old Master indices show price spikes in 1990 and a second dramatic rise in 1998. The top 25 per cent of works by value have produced the greatest increases in these two years. All the Old Master markets by sector and percentage show a steady or dramatic increase from 2005 until 2012, while the top quartile has almost doubled the value of the 1990 and 1998 spikes.

The other market that has commanded high prices in recent years is the Chinese Imperial ceramics market and in particular pieces from the Ming and Qing dynasties. Yet overall performance has slipped or remained flat across two key indices from the beginning of 2008. Chinese ceramics in general rose consistently from 1976 to early 2009, at which point the index started to slip. The top 25 per cent has continued to rise throughout this period. The middle 80 per cent has risen more gradually during this time frame. The top 25 per cent fell after March 2009 and the middle 80 per cent has remained flat since 2007. This evidence, the result of the 'random sample' or 'basket' methodology employed by Art Market Report, underlines the problems in gauging the performance of even a relatively homogenous commodity like Chinese ceramics. In short, can a single object be indicative of the performance of a group of similar articles? Can the results of one sale for one item be generalised to refer to all items in any one particular sub-sector? The problems in measurement are exacerbated when one turns to unique artefacts like paintings. There have been exceptionally high headline prices achieved in this market. Alice Cheng, the sister of the late Hong Kong dealer Robert Chang, paid $32.6 million for a Qianlong (1711–99), double gourd-shaped *famille rose* vase in 2010 at Sotheby's Hong Kong. The Shanghai heiress had bought and donated another *famille rose* vase from the same period to the Shanghai Museum. She paid $5.29 million for that piece in 2002. These two price points contradict the top 25 per cent index and demonstrate how difficult it is to generalise results. It is preferable, in theory, to adopt a repeat sales methodology (see Beautiful Asset Management LLC) to plot prices movements, although in practice the length of time between resales skews the significance of the data.

It is possible that the prices for *mille fleurs* Chinese ceramics reached a peak in 2008, as the indices suggest, although an exceptional piece will always excite interest. The price of $27 million achieved for the flat, flower-shaped, porcelain Ru brush-washer at Sotheby's, Hong Kong in 2012, pushed to this level by eight bidders, against an estimate of $7.7 million – $10.3 million, is just one example of the masterpiece effect. This result has two implications; first, when a truly great and rare piece of art comes to market, there is no price ceiling and second, Chinese government policy to protect national antiquities, endorsed at the National People's Congress in March 2012, is adding fuel to the already hot Chinese antiques market. There are 85 extant examples of Ru of which only five are in private hands. A flat Ru dish was sold by Christie's in New York in 1992 for $1.54 million (today $2.29 million). The late Julian Thompson, former Chairman of Sotheby's, Asia (1941–2011), estimated its value in 2005 to be $4.5 million. Effectively, the value of Ru trebled between 1992 and 2005 and increased in value sixfold between 2005 and 2012.

An annual conference organised by Deloitte in 2011 in Miami placed the notion of art and investment centre stage. The resulting Art & Finance Report (2011) drew on current academic research, notably the findings of Michael Moses, whose 'robust repeat sales methodology', which included data from China, seemed to be the chosen industry methodology for indices if not for valuation. Moses concluded that 'their annual art index values outperformed S&P Total Return Equity Index between 2000 and September 2011'. The report further concluded that the art market decline at the beginning of the millennium was shallower and the subsequent growth from 2003 until the peak in 2008 more marked than equities. This pattern continued in 2010 and 2011, over which period art and antiques outperformed the equity indices once more. The findings appear to support the discoveries of a previous study conducted by Deloitte in 2009, which pointed to a marked increase in the performance of art (especially contemporary art) from 2005–9. It also confirms that art and antiques offer greater downside protection than financial products. This gives the investor countercyclical security against a downturn in the stock market in particular. It means that when the economic situation deteriorates, the value of art is left relatively unaffected, although the degree to which this holds true, and the length of time that art effectively decouples itself from the wider economy, is much disputed.

Half the respondents in the Deloitte 2011 Report thought art to be a pure investment. Most found valuation and the assessment of downside risk very difficult to accept. The report identified perhaps the most troublesome difficulty of art as an asset: liquidity. In short, if there isn't a buyer for the work no amount of data generated by indices will find you one. Here the report fights shy of highlighting the many examples of works of art that remain 'on the shelf' because tastes have changed. It also ignores the impact of re-attribution on the price and security of a work of art. Due diligence can offset a great many risks, but not these two. There is an added risk that 'burned' works (art and antiques that have failed to sell at auction on numerous occasions) will not find a buyer. In response to this, the report could have looked at reserve-free sales. In theory and practice there is always a price for an object, and there are markets to deal with just about any item. This upsets the appraisal-based bias and investment incentive of art and antiques, but it does at least give the investor a get-out-of-jail card. Data veracity is particularly problematic in China. The Chinese Association for Auctioneers suggests that up to half the works that sold for over $1 million dollars in China have remained unpaid. It is a percentage that highlights the worldwide problem of data unreliability in the art market.

Despite the difficulties encountered by the art investor, the art fund market has grown. The Deloitte 2011 Report estimates that there are as many as 44 art funds and investment trusts, with 21 in China alone. There is even talk that it was the Zhong Yi Da Cheng Art Fund (launched by the Hunan TV and Broadcast Intermediary Co.) that bought *A Long Life, A Peaceful World* by Qi Baishi (1864–1957) for a record $65 million in May 2011, although this has since been attributed to a private buyer who failed to pay. Any investor should be wary of unregulated art funds, and South Korea provides a cautionary tale. In her dissertation on 'The Rise and Fall of Art Funds in Korea between 2006 and 2008' (Sotheby's Institute of Art) Minjung Kim suggests that a combination of factors led to the collapse of most art funds: a global market downturn, corruption within the Korean art market and the levying of a capital gains tax on art (20 per cent tax on profits made from art in excess of $60,000). The Korean art fund market also suffered, according to Kim, from a lack of transparency and a knowledge deficit. There were negligible safeguards in the structure whereby dealers recommeneded works for accession to managers of funds including Good Morning Shinhan Securities, Golden Bridge Asset Management and Korea Investment. But there are successful funds, such as the Fine Art Fund Group. Luxembourg Elite Advisors, which launched funds in wine and watches a few years ago, has opened a third in precious stones and jewellery, feeding off the new passion for SWAG (silver, wine, art and gold). Other notable funds introduced to the market in recent years are: Artemundi (2009) and the Brazilian Golden Art Fund (2011), managing a total of $340 million. Art lenders, like the American-based Art Assure and European PlatinumArt and Borro have entered the fray, providing secured lending and guarantees for works sold at auction to art collectors, established galleries, auction houses and global investors. The securitisation of art comes hard on the heels of its financialisation. Once art is regarded as a financial asset capable of capital gains, lenders will appear, willing to lend against art, secure in the knowledge that the value of art may rise but it will be very unlikely to fall to zero. This might of course be a logical fallacy.

An even more surprising dimension to the revolution affecting the art market is the art exchange. The first regulated multilateral trading facility, SplitArt, failed to secure the approval of the Luxembourg Financial Services Authority. It aspired, according to its general manager, to open the market by offering blind bidding Art Certificates (shares) in single works of art. In theory the art exchange frees the investor from the onerous and at times treacherous task of due diligence, but there is a danger that if left underregulated, the value of the work can be manipulated. The Achilles heel of this exchange afflicts all such endeavours; it is very difficult to own fragments of a commodity that is varied. In the case of a landscape painting for example, one collector may own a square centimetre of sky and another a similar amount of land; how then can either of these different fragments be collateralised in the event of a desire to sell? Both must hold dissimilar values. The essential problem remains the disconnection between the actual market value of the art and its notional share price value. This proved to be the undoing of an art exchange in China. The share price of two paintings traded on the Tianjin Art Exchange rose 1,700 per cent in a couple of months, valuing one painting at 52 times the highest price achieved by that artist at auction, prompting a leading figure in the Chinese art world to comment wryly that shared ownership in a painting implied that you might be the proud owner of a single brush mark. In 2011 the Tianjin Municipal Authority stepped in to suspend trading in the two pictures. It has since introduced daily price limits and maximum account thresholds to the exchange. The problems inherent in the China art market were revealed at Deloitte EU-China Cultural Dialogue in Luxembourg in October 2011. The conference concluded that the China market turnover has been over-estimated (Artprice attributed 39 per cent of this market to China in 2011), that it lacked diversity and that it had underdeveloped legal and regulatory frameworks. It was critical of market integrity and expertise and feared speculation. These are key concerns for a market keen to encourage non-industry investors. Since 2011 the China art market has been in decline, primarily as a result of investigations into tax evasion, money-laundering and corruption. All markets are subject to government intervention and the political mood.

Art is a rewarding asset that can produce substantial capital gains and might offer downside protection. It appears to be weakly correlated to most assets, but corresponds more closely to the performance of art and gold. It is, in the main, a non-fungible asset, and it is from this quality that it derives much of its value. It is, on the other hand, extremely expensive to acquire and hold, financially sterile and subject to changes in fashion. Finally, art is subject to the consequences of re-attribution, which can work in its favour and to its detriment.

Iain Robertson

Bibliography

Ashenfelter, Orley, 'Art Auctions', in R. Towse (ed.), *A Handbook of Cultural Economics,* Edward Elgar, 2003, pp 32–40

Campbell, R., and Adriano Picinati di Torcello, *Performance and Correlation of Art as an Alternative Asset Class During the Current Financial Crisis,* Deloitte Luxembourg, 2009

Coffman, Richard, 'Art Investment and Asymmetrical Information', *Journal of Cultural Economics,* no.20, 1991, pp 1–24

Duthy, Robin, 'Various Indices and Information', *Art Market Research,* 2013, www.artmarketresearch.com

Gerlis, Melanie, *Art as an Investment? A Survey of Comparative Assets,* Lund Humphries, 2014

Hoeltgen, Thierry, Adriano Picinati di Torcello and Anders Petterson, *Art & Finance Report Dec 2011,* Deloitte Luxembourg, 2011

Horowitz, Noah, *Art of the Deal: Contemporary Art in a Global Financial Market,* Princeton University Press, 2011

Hutter, Michael, C. Knebel and G. Pietzner, 'Two Games in Town: A Comparison of Dealer and Auction Prices in Contemporary Visual Arts Markets', *Journal of Cultural Economics,* vol.31, no.4, pp 247–61

McAndrew, Clare, *Fine Art and High Finance: Expert Advice on the Economics of Ownership,* Bloomberg Press, 2010

Mei, Jianping, and Michael Moses, 'Art as an Investment and the Underperformance of Masterpieces', *SSRN Electronic Journal,* 2002

Mei, Jianping and Michael Moses, 'Vested Interest and Biased Price Estimates: Evidence from an Auction Market', *Journal of Finance,* vol.60, no.5, 2005, pp 2409–35

Reitlinger, G., *The Economics of Taste: The Rise and Fall of Picture Prices 1760–1960,* Barrie and Rockliff, 1961

Robertson, Iain, *Understanding Art Markets: Inside the World of Art and Business,* Routledge, 2015

PRIVATE MUSEUMS
AND THE ART MARKET

The mushrooming growth of so-called private museums since the turn of this century is a phenomenon worth looking at, as it is so reflective of the art market in general. The creation of private museums – that is, publicly accessible spaces that are funded by an individual and primarily show that person's art – is not new. Several of today's most respected institutions started out as vehicles to display one collection, such as New York's Frick Collection, Florence's Uffizi Gallery and Sir John Soane's Museum in London. What is new, however, is the pace at which such museums are appearing.

The numbers are not completely consistent. The 'Private Art Museum Report' by Larry's List (2015) records 317 private museums and spaces worldwide; in the same year the 'BMW Art Guide by Independent Collectors' reports 236. However, the rate of growth since 2000 is indisputable. Three-quarters of those on the BMW list opened since 2000; a fifth of those on Larry's List since 2010. All data records that China was responsible for a very high proportion of private museum openings during those five years. Many private museums that are just a few years old have already gained some institutional status within the contemporary art world. They include the 2014 openings of the Louis Vuitton Foundation in Paris, founded by Bernard Arnault (b.1949), and the Yuz Museum in Shanghai, founded by Budi Tek (b.1957). The new Garage Museum in Moscow opened in 2015, founded by Dasha Zhukova (b.1981). That these museums exist is, on the face of it, beneficial to a wider public, which gets to see more art and perhaps enjoy the more eclectic taste of one or two individuals. However, the philosophies behind them and the impact they are having on the art world at large – including the heavy bias towards contemporary art – do also raise wider cultural and ethical issues.

For the sake of brevity, the term 'private museum' is used in the discussion as the opposite of a 'public museum', which in turn is used to describe a museum that receives any national, state funding. This is broadly the case, though in reality the lines here are more blurred than they appear.

One of the key drivers behind the building of museums to show private purchases has been the worldwide growth of individual wealth, and wealth inequality, since 2000. In 2015, Forbes recorded 1,826 dollar billionaires worldwide, up from 1,645 the previous year. In 2000, there were 322 dollar billionaires recorded on Forbes' annual list. China, Nigeria and Russia are among the countries in which billionaire growth has been the most marked, though the United States consistently produces a very high number. At the same time the growth in the number of wealthy individuals who participate directly in the art market's visible arenas – auction rooms, art fairs and most other commercial and social events – has been marked.

Individual collectors have subsequently grown in status within the wider art world. The annual *Art Review Power 100* ranking of all art players included 15 private individuals in 2015, all but one of whom run or are soon to run a private museum – and *all* of whom buy contemporary art. Such rankings (and *Artnews* has run a dedicated list of the top 200 collectors since 1990) have undoubtedly contributed to a certain competitiveness within collecting circles and the growing distinctions between 'good' and 'bad' collectors that the art market likes to apply. One of the key ways for a collector to pull rank is not just to buy art but to show it, in a dedicated, starchitect-designed 'museum'. There are, of course, other advantages that individuals cite for having a more public space to show their works, some of which ring truer than others.

From a practical point of view, a museum overcomes the space constraints of even the priciest homes. The overwhelming amount of supply that clamours for buyers' attention, particularly in the unlimited contemporary art market, needs to hang somewhere. The works also keep getting bigger, partly in order to stand out from this very noisy crowd. And hanging isn't always the end game: sculpture, video and performance pieces abound, and a huge range of conceptual and multimedia works are entering the market's mainstream. One of the most popular and distinct sections at an art fair is Unlimited at Art Basel, a hall filled with larger-than-life and multi-faceted works, which launched in 2000. Exacerbating the sheer amount and size of work on offer is the fact that a 'good' collector is not meant to sell; or certainly not for at least ten years. (See 'Art as Investment').

Another of the art market's codes that a private museum helps to unlock is getting to the top of the list for new works by sought-after artists. Dealers, who aim to control their contemporary artists' markets as much as possible, have found that one way to engineer this is to 'place' their works – that is, to pick and choose who is able to buy them. Historically, a public museum has been top of this list, but this is an increasingly limited field, not least because of the high prices that major contemporary art now commands. Liza Essers, who runs South Africa's commercial Goodman Gallery, told *The Art Newspaper* that for the Art Basel Miami Beach fair in 2013, 'I focus more on private collections when making my selection'. Public museum curators were still important, she said, but the best she could hope for was to 'get them interested in giving our artists a show in the US'.

The growing exploration of the investment potential of art also plays a part in the private museum game. While nearly all private collectors, especially those who run museums, are quick to deny any financial incentive to their activity, they are rarely unaware of the economics. Private collectors who are able to lend their works to public museum exhibitions will almost certainly see these works go up in value. Such shows provide the ultimate cultural validation in a crowded field. This has presented an ethical issue for the public museums, which have experienced an increasing number of 'show and sell' situations – that is when a work is sold very soon after appearing in a museum exhibition. (Or even, as in the case of a Christopher Wool heavily promoted by the Guggenheim, New York in 2014, just before a museum exhibition opens.) By showing work instead in their own private museum, a collector can, to some extent, reap the same benefit without testing the art world's ethical code (though some private museums are set up to restrict outright selling). Moreover, it isn't just one or two works that benefit from the cultural, and therefore economic, capital of being in a public exhibition; it could be dozens, or even an entire collection.

Collections that have grown enormously in value, and whose founders have emerged as tastemakers, include that of Don and Mera Rubell, who formed their Miami family collection in 1964. They have supported internationally renowned artists including Richard Prince (b.1949), Jeff Koons and Cindy Sherman and, more recently, have helped make the careers of and markets for, for example, Elad Lassry (b.1977), Zhang Huang (b.1965), and the *wunderkind* Oscar Murillo (b.1986). There is also a more tangible financial benefit to owning and running private museums though, again, very few collectors cite this as a reason behind their decision. While they are generally managed as not-for-profit businesses, this is usually done through a separate legal ownership, such as a charitable trust or foundation, which offers tax breaks. These are different in each country or state – as indeed are the relative tax advantages of lending works to public museums – but they offer a collector control, plus a financial benefit. In the US, where government agencies fund a considerably lower percentage of museums, the tax breaks offered to collectors are generally more advantageous than elsewhere. For the founder-collector of a private museum, these can extend to being able to deduct the full market value of any art and other assets that they 'donate' to their foundation. Plus there are additional tax advantages that govern maintaining and buying its art. Scrutiny of the public benefit of such breaks was intensified in December 2015 when the chairman of the Senate Finance Committee in the US wrote to 11 private museums requesting information on attendance, opening hours, trustees and grant-making activities. The letter expressed concern that some institutions 'offer minimal benefit to the public' and was part of a wider enquiry into preferential tax treatments. In May 2016, the enquiry's findings were sent to the US government's Inland Revenue Service.

Despite such concerns, private museum owners cite some compelling philanthropic advantages of their presence on the art world map. For a start, it must not be forgotten that, despite the possible tax advantages, these enterprises are not cheap. The Brazilian mining magnate Bernardo Paz (b.1949) reportedly spends between $60 m and $70 million a year on his Inhotim art complex, which includes a botanical garden with 1,400 species of tree as well as immersive, expansive works by artists including Doug Aitken (b.1968) and Hélio Oiticica (1937–80). Showing works that otherwise wouldn't get an airing – and which can have a very distinct aesthetic – is almost undeniably in the (cultural) public interest. In countries where the nationally promoted art is restricted and even censored, a private museum can also provide a much-needed alternative platform.

Through all regions, most private museum owners devote considerable resources to the educational possibilities that can go alongside their display. The seemingly tireless Patrizia Re Rebaudengo (b.1959), who shows her international contemporary art collection at the vast Fondazione Sandretto Re Rebaudengo in Turin, points out that when her space was founded in 1995 there were very few other places to see contemporary art in Italy. (Maxxi in Rome was the country's first national museum dedicated to contemporary and opened in 2010.) She emphasises the benefits to living artists and the public and says that her foundation currently works with 20,000 students a year, a number she sees as growing considerably, as well as offering public learning programmes. The foundation's educational reach also includes training curators and conservators and residency programmes for artists. Presenting themselves as operating a very twenty-first-century model, private museum owners also highlight the speed at which they can make decisions as a distinct advantage over the public museums, which are bound by much more red tape and collective decision-making – although it could be argued that such formalities exist for good reasons.

Another positive outcome of the growing number of private museums is the ability to create networks and exchanges that, again, are less cumbersome to effect. For example, in 2011, the curator, broadcaster and Sinophile Philip Dodd (b.1949) launched a closed-door Private Museum Summit at the ArtBasel Hong Kong fair. The summit has had several iterations since, but is now the Global Private Museum Network, and aims to generate conversations and share expertise, funding strategies and even works and exhibitions between the sporadic individuals that own private museums around the world. Its members include the Rubell Family Collection in Miami, the Fondazione Sandretto Re Rebaudengo in Turin and the Long and Yuz museums in Shanghai. Such networks have a particular currency for players in less traditional art world arenas, such as in China, which can lack the institutional infrastructure that otherwise brings connections.

Whether or not Dodd's initiative will have any tangible effects remains to be seen, though its participants speak of it highly. It certainly chimes with the way in which today's wealthy like to conduct their lives, business, interests and, seemingly, philanthropy: not as individuals hemmed in by national borders, but as part of a club of similarly minded (and minted) individuals. Thus the creation of private museums becomes a defining characteristic that they all share. As Chrystia Freeland writes in her incisive 2012 book *The Plutocrats*:

> ... whether you got your start in western Siberia or the American Midwest, once you join the super-elite you patronize the same dentist, interior designer, art curator. That's how, from the inside, the plutonomy becomes a cozy global village.

Despite the private museum owners' ambition to be eclectic and original, the elite social network is a powerful yet uniform force, so certain artists thus become the approved international contemporary artists; certain styles are preferred; certain dealers and art advisers supported. American artists, particularly Andy Warhol and the Minimalists Donald Judd (1928–94) and Sol LeWitt (1928–2007) – appear in more than half the collections recorded by Larry's List. Homogeneity begins to creep in. At the same time, the state-backed museums haven't been helping themselves as the lines between the public and the private are increasingly blurred. For Tate Modern in London to run, in 2012, a major five-month solo exhibition dedicated to Damien Hirst that was sponsored by the Qatar Museums Authority, which owns several pricey works by the artist, is ethically questionable. Other institutions have hosted exhibitions dedicated to private collections, whose selection has also raised red flags. Furthermore, the public museums carry the greatest responsibility, because their visitor numbers are so much higher. Tate Modern had 4.7 million visitors in 2015, the seventh highest in the world, according to *The Art Newspaper*'s annual attendance survey. Only three private museums – the Saatchi Gallery, London (1.6 million visitors) the Foundation Louis Vuitton, Paris (1 million) and the Ullens Center for Contemporary Art, Beijing (760,000) – made it into the top 100. Larry's List finds that just over a third of private museums have over 20,000 visitors per year, its top threshold. It should be noted, also, that private museums are a tiny proportion of the total number of institutions worldwide. As such, these can be the most vulnerable. In

February 2016, one of France's rare and respected private museums, the Paris Pinacothèque, announced a sudden decision to close because of a drop in attendance following the terror attacks in the city in 2015. Its founder, Marc Restellini (b.1964), told *Le Monde* that when the going got tough France's state museums, which don't pay rent or value-added-tax on ticket sales, were at a considerable advantage.

It is not a black-and-white situation, however. Writing in *The Art Newspaper* in 2008, the art consultant Adrian Ellis summed up how 'the increasingly complex and conflicted relationship between active private collectors and public museums are all manifestations of large-scale change in the institutional ecology of art'. The debates will rage on as the growth of private museums – more a symptom than a cause of this century's conspicuous consumption, self-motivation and wealth creation – is not going away fast.

Melanie Gerlis

Bibliography

Adam, Georgina, *Big Bucks: The Explosion of the Art Market in the 21st Century*, Lund Humphries, 2014

BMW Group (ed.), 'BMW Art Guide by Independent Collectors', Hatje Cantz, 2015

Burns, Charlotte, Gareth Harris and Julia Michalska, 'The Substance Beneath the Style', *The Art Newspaper*, Art Basel Miami Beach daily edition, 5 December 2013, pp 1–2

Cohen, Patricia, 'Writing Off the Warhol Next Door', *The New York Times*, 10 January 2015, www.nytimes.com/ 2015/01/11/business/art-collectors-gain-tax-benefits-from-private-museums. html?_r=0

Ellis, Adrian, 'The Problem with Privately Funded Museums', *The Art Newspaper*, issue 188, February 2008, p.24

Freeland, Chrystia, *Plutocrats: The Rise of the New Global Super-Rich and the Fall of Everyone Else*, Allen Lane, 2012

Gnyp, Marta, *The Shift: Art and the Rise to Power of Contemporary Collectors*, Art and Theory Publishing, 2015

Halperin, Julia, and Javier Pes, 'Public Benefit of US Private Museums under
    Scrutiny', *The Art Newspaper*, Art Basel Miami Beach daily edition,
    5 December 2015, p.2

Jardonnet, Emmanuelle, 'La Pinacothèque de Paris ferme ses portes', *Le Monde*,
    12 February 2016, www.lemonde.fr/arts/article/2016/02/12/en-redressement-
    judiciaire-la-pinacotheque-de-paris-annonce-sa-fermeture_4864621_
    1655012.html

Larry's List and Art Market Monitor of Artron (eds), 'Private Art Museum
    Report', Modern Arts Publishing, January 2016

Power 100, 2015, *Art Review*, available at http://artreview.com/power_100/

Renneboog, Luc, and Christophe Spaenjers, 'Art and Money', in *Yale School
    of Management Working Paper*, nos 09–26, Yale School of Management,
    28 April 2010

'Visitor Figures 2015', *The Art Newspaper*, issue 278, April 2016

BIBLIOGRAPHY

Since the turn of the millennium, and the dramatic shift in the scale and scope of the art market, many publications have sought to consider the impact of this phenomenon on both the art world and the art market – particularly the unparalleled expansion of the contemporary art market. Sarah Thornton's *Seven Days in the Art World* (2008) is an ethnographic analysis of seven key narratives or art world structures – presented as 'days': the auction, the critic, the fair, the prize, the magazine, the studio visit and the biennale. During this period a number of studies have focused on the art market. Georgina Adam's *Big Bucks: the Explosion of the Art Market in the 21st Century* (2014) examines the current state of the art market and considers auction houses, dealers, artists and 'taste-makers' along with key determinants in a changing marketplace with an emphasis on contemporary art and the rise of art fairs, online sales, the impact of emerging markets and new buyers and issues around transparency and market regulation.

The growth of art market studies as an academic field, and more particularly of art business as an academic discipline predominantly based in the social sciences alongside cultural and visual art studies, has witnessed a corresponding increase in academic articles, books and conferences. Since 2000 numerous academic articles have considered the economics of the art market. These papers can be found in, for example, the *Journal of Cultural Economics*, *Poetics*, the *International Journal of Cultural Management*, the *International Journal of Cultural Heritage and Management*, the *Journal of Financial and Quantitative Analysis*, the *American Economic Review*, the *European Economic Review* and the *Harvard Business Review*.

As well as the economics of art, numerous writers in the Academy have focused on art market investment, including Clare McAndrew, whose *The Art Economy: An Investor's Guide to the Art Market* was published in 2007. McAndrew now publishes annual reports on the art market that are invaluable for both researchers and professionals in the field. Since 2011 Deloitte has published *Art and Finance* Reports. Other reports of note are those published by Art Tactic, which adopt a more distinctive and more qualitative approach. Jianping Mei and Michael Moses considered 'Art as an Investment and the Underperformance of Masterpieces' in 2002 and more recently have followed this up with an index of sales/prices, the

Mei Moses Art Indices, which consider historical investment and art as an asset class based on auction transactions. In *Art of the Deal: Contemporary Art in a Global Financial Market* (2011), Noah Horowitz analyses the dynamics of the international art market and investment with a particular focus on contemporary art. Interestingly, he considers performance and conceptual art, both of which are more difficult to commodify.

Olav Velthius's *Talking Prices: Symbolic Meanings of Prices on the Market for Contemporary Art* (2005) builds on ideas first expressed by Pierre Bourdieu, placing a great emphasis on symbolic capital. As well as a theoretical approach, his handling of the issues surrounding price and value is sociological and reminds us that the new academic field of art business is located more in the social sciences and humanities than it is in the field of business studies. Anna Dempster's *Risk and Uncertainty in the Art World* (2014) is an edited volume of essays examining risk and uncertainty in relation to the art market. The text engages critically with a topic of continuing concern particularly in light of the 2007–11 global recession. Melanie Gerlis's *Art as an Investment? A Survey of Comparative Assets* (2014) brings us further up to date in its examination of art's value as an asset, comparing it with other types of asset and in the process considering the pros and cons of art as an investment.

With respect to the study of art business, James Goodwin's *The International Art Markets, The Essential Guide for Collectors and Investors* (2009) represents a new and distinctive approach to art market studies with 43 entries on different countries/geographic areas. The introduction is as much an introduction to art business as it is to the various workings of the art market. Here Goodwin considers primary and secondary markets, notions of value, art fairs, collecting, art and investment and, briefly, sections on law and tax. Iain Robertson and Derrick Chong's *The Art Business* (2008) is one of the rare texts which engages directly with and analyses the complex field of art business. While the approach is primarily from an economic perspective it is firmly rooted in the social sciences and cultural studies and significantly includes essays on law and ethics. Similarly Iain Robertson's *Understanding Art Markets: Inside the World of Art and Business* (2016), while focusing on the market, also engages with the larger art world including law, ethics and the public sector. Robertson has presented a third way, which depends on the interpretation of changes outside the industry; the impact, in short of tangible external forces on the art market.

Jos Hackforth-Jones and Iain Robertson

Art Business and the Art Market

Adam, Georgina, *Big Bucks: The Explosion of the Art Market in the 21st Century*, Lund Humphries, 2014

Bamberger, Alan, *The Art of Buying Art*, Gordon's Art Reference Inc, 2007

Becker, Howard S., *Art Worlds*, University of California Press, 1982

Boswell, David and Jessica Evans, *Representing the Nation: A Reader: Histories, Heritage and Museums*, Routledge, 2007

Bowness, Alan, *The Conditions of Success: How the Modern Artist Rises to Fame*, Thames and Hudson, 1989

Buck, Louisa, *Market Matters: The Dynamics of the Contemporary Art Market*, Arts Council England, 2004

Buck, Louisa and Judith Greer, *Owning Art: The Contemporary Art Collector's Handbook*, Cultureshock Media Ltd, London, 2006

Cuno, James, *Whose Muse? Art Museums and the Public Trust*, Princeton University Press, 2006

Chong, Derrick, *Arts Management*, Routledge, 2007

de Montebello, Philippe, 'Art Museums: Inspiring Public Trust' in J. Cuno, *Whose Muse? Art Museums and the Public Trust*, Princeton University Press, 2006

Dempster, Anna (ed.), *Risk and Uncertainty in the Art World*, Bloomsbury, 2014

Ferguson, Niall, *The Cash Nexus: Money and Power in the Modern World 1700–2000*, Allen Lane/ Penguin Books, 2001

Foster, Hal, *The Art-Architecture Complex*, Verso, 2013

Galbraith, John Kenneth, *A Short History of Financial Euphoria*, Penguin, 1994

Gerlis, Melanie, *Art as an Investment? A Survey of Comparative Assets*, Lund Humphries, 2014

Gigerenzer, Gerd, *Reckoning with Risk: Learning to Live with Uncertainty*, Penguin, 2002

Goodwin, James (ed.), *The International Art Markets: The Essential Guide for Collectors and Investors*, Kogan Page, 2008

Grampp, William D., *Pricing the Priceless: Art, Artists and Economics*, Basic Books, 1989

Hall, Stuart, 'Culture, Community, Nation', *Cultural Studies*, 1993, vol.7, no.3, Routledge in association with the Open University

Heilbrun, Richard, *The Economics of Art and Culture*, Cambridge University Press, 2001

Herbert, John, *Inside Christie's*, St Martin's Press, 1990

Hermann, Frank, *Sotheby's: Portrait of an Auction House*, Chatto & Windus, 1980

Hook, Philip, *Breakfast at Sotheby's: An A–Z of the Art World*, Particular Books, 2013

Horowitz, Noah, *Art of the Deal: Contemporary Art in a Global Financial Market*,
    Princeton University Press, 2011

King, Elaine A., and Gail Levin (eds), *Ethics and the Visual Arts*, Skyhorse
    Publishing, Inc., 2013.

Mason, Christopher, *The Art of the Steal: inside the Sotheby's-Christie's Auction
    House Scandal*, Putnam Publishing Group, 2004

McAndrew, Clare, *The Art Economy: An Investor's Guide to the Art Market*,
    The Liffey Press, 2007

McAndrew, Clare, *Fine Art and High Finance: Expert Advice on the Economics
    of Ownership*, Bloomberg Press, 2010

Moulin, Raymonde, *The French Art Market: a Sociological View*, Rutgers, 1987

Reitlinger, Gerald, *The Economics of Taste*: *the Rise and Fall of Picture Prices
    1760–1960*, Barrie and Rockliff, 1961

Robertson, Iain, *A New Art from Emerging Markets*, Lund Humphries, 2011

Robertson, Iain, *Understanding Art Markets: Inside the World of Art and Business*,
    Routledge, 2016

Robertson, Iain, and Derrick Chong, *The Art Business*, Routledge, 2008

Sebald, Winfried G., *On the Natural History of Destruction*, The Modern Library, 2004

Skaterschikov, Sergey, *Skate's Art Investment Handbook: The Comprehensive
    Guide to Investing in the Global and Art Services Market*, McGraw Hill, 2009,
    see esp. chapters 3 and 4

Thornton, Sarah, *Seven Days in the Art World*, Granta, 2008

Velthuis, Olav, *Talking Prices: Symbolic Meanings of Prices on the Market for
    Contemporary Art*, Princeton University Press, 2005

Velthuis, Olav, and Stefano B. Curioni (eds), *Cosmopolitan Canvases: the
    Globalization of Markets for Contemporary Art*, Oxford University Press, 2015

Von Holst, Niels, *Creators, Collectors and Connoisseurs: The Anatomy of Artistic
    Taste from Antiquity to the Present Day*, Book Club Associates, 1976

Art and the Law

Christopherson, Tom, 'Art Market Risk and Complexity: An Insider's View'
    in Anna Dempster (ed.) *Risk and Uncertainty in the Art World*, Bloomsbury,
    2014

Harvey, Brian W., and Franklin Meisel, *Auctions Law and Practice,*
    Oxford University Press, 3rd edn, 2006

Prowda, Judith B., *Visual Arts and the Law*, Lund Humphries in association
    with Sotheby's Institute of Art, 2013

Stokes, Simon, *Art and Copyright,* Hart Publishing, 2nd edn, 2012

ARTICLES

Adil Essajee, 'Commissions – The Best Kept Secret?', Withers LLP, Art and
    Cultural Assets Spring 2013
Pierre Valentin, 'The Price of Confidentiality', Constantine Cannon LLP, 2014
    http://www.artatlaw.com/archives/the-price-of-confidentiality
http://www.withersworldwide.com/system/files/2380/original/ACA_
    Newsletter_Spring_2013.pdf

Authenticity

Aldrich, Megan, and Jos Hackforth-Jones (eds), *Art and Authenticity*, Lund
    Humphries, 2012/Sotheby's Institute of Art, 2012
Moore, Abigail Harrison, *Fraud, Fakery and False Business: Rethinking the
    Shräger v. Dighton 'Old Furniture Case'*, Continuum, 2011
Spencer, Ronald D. (ed.), *The Expert versus the Object: Judging Fakes and False
    Attributions in the Visual Arts*, Oxford University Press, 2004
Tromp, Henk, *A Real Van Gogh: How the Art World Struggles with Truth*,
    Amsterdam University Press, 2010
Tummers, Anna, *The Eye of the Connoisseur: Authenticating Paintings by
    Rembrandt and His Contemporaries*, Getty Publications, 2011

RECENT LEGAL CASES

Avrora Fine Arts Investment Ltd v Christie, Manson & Woods Ltd [2012]
    EWHC 2198 (Ch)
Baron Coleridge of Ottery St. Mary v Sotheby's [2012] EWHC 370 (Ch)
Drake v Thos. Agnew & Sons Ltd [2002] EWHC 294 (QB)
Lancelot Thwaytes v Sotheby's [2015] EWHC 36 (Ch)
Taylor Lynne Thomson v Christie, Manson & Woods Ltd [2005] EWCA Civ 555
    (Court of Appeal)

Art Fairs

Barragán, Paco, *The Art Fair Age*, Charta, 2008
Lind, Maria, and Olav Velthuis (eds), *Contemporary Art and Its Commercial Markets:
    A Report on Current Conditions and Future Scenarios*, Sternberg Press, 2012
Moeran, Brian, and Jesper Strandgaard Pedersen (eds), *Negotiating Values
    in the Creative Industries: Fairs, Festivals and Competitive Events*,
    Cambridge University Press, 2011

O'Reilly, Daragh, Ruth Rentschler and Theresa A. Kirchner (eds), *The Routledge Companion to Arts Marketing,* Routledge, 2013

ARTICLES

Quemin, Alain, 'International Contemporary Art Fairs in a 'Globalised' Art Market', *European Societies*, 2013, vol.15, issue 2, pp 162–77

Museums, Collecting, Curating and Display

Altshuler, Bruce (ed.), *Collecting the New: Museums and Contemporary Art*, Princeton University Press, 2007

Anderson, Robert, *The Great Court and The British Museum*, British Museum Press, 2000

Barker, Emma, *Contemporary Culture of Display*, Yale University Press, 1999

Buck, Louisa and Daniel McClean, *Commissioning Contemporary Art: A Handbook for Curators, Collectors and Artists*, Thames & Hudson, 2012

Buck, Louisa and Judith Greer, *Owning Art: The Contemporary Art Collector's Handbook*, Cultureshock Media Ltd, London, 2006

Camber, Richard (ed.), *Collectors and Collections*, British Museum Press, 1977

Cabanne, Pierre, *The Great Collectors*, Cassell, 1963

Caygill, Marjorie and Neil MacGregor, *The British Museum: 250 Years*, British Museum Press, 2003

Cuno, James (ed.), *Whose Muse? Art Museums and the Public Trust*, Princeton University Press, 2006

Duncan, Carol, *Civilizing Rituals: Inside Public Art Museums*, Routledge, 1995

Elsner, John, and Roger Cardinal (eds), *The Cultures of Collecting*, Reaktion, 1994

Greenberg, Reesa, Bruce Ferguson and Sandy Nairne, *Thinking About Exhibitions*, Routledge, 1996

Hooper-Greenhill, Eilean, *The Educational Role of the Museum*, Routledge, 1999

Ingamells, John, *The 3rd Marquess of Hertford (1777–1842) as a Collector*, Wallace Collection, 1983

Macdonald, Sharon, *A Companion to Museum Studies*, Wiley-Blackwell, 2011

Mallett, Donald, *The Greatest Collector: Lord Hertford and the Founding of the Wallace Collection*, Macmillan, 1979

Marincola, Paula (ed.), *What Makes a Great Exhibition?*, University of the Arts, Philadelphia Exhibitions Initiative, 2007

Marstine, Janet (ed.), *The Routledge Companion to Museum Ethics: Redefining Ethics for the 21st Century Museum*, Routledge, 2011

McClellan, Andrew, *Art and its Publics: Museum Studies at the Millennium*,
   Wiley-Blackwell, 2003

McClellan, Andrew, *The Art Museum: From Boullée to Bilbao*, University
   of California Press, 2008

Miller, Edward, *That Noble Cabinet: A History of The British Museum*, Andre
   Deutsch, 1973

Mordaunt Crook, Joseph, *The British Museum: A Case Study in Architectural
   Politics*, Pelican, 1973

O'Doherty, Brian, *Inside the White Cube: The Ideology of the Gallery Space*,
   University of California, 2000

O'Neill, Paul, *The Culture of Curating and the Curating of Culture(s)*, MIT Press,
   2012

Paul, Carole, *The First Modern Museums of Art: the Birth of an Institution
   in 18th and early 19th Century Europe*, Getty Publications, 2012

Pearce, Susan M., *Museums, Objects and Collections*, Smithsonian Institution,
   1992

Pearce, Susan M., *The Collector's Voice: Critical Readings in the Practice
   of Collecting. Imperial Voices*, Ashgate, vol.3, 2002

Pointon, Marcia, *Art Apart: Art Institutions and Ideology across England and
   North America*, Manchester University Press, 1994

Prior, Nick, *Museums and Modernity: Art Galleries and the Making of Modern
   Culture*, Berg, 2002

Rozell, Mary, *The Art Collector's Handbook: A Guide to Collection Management
   and Care* (Handbooks in International Art Business), Lund Humphries, 2013

Sandell, Richard (ed.), *Museums, Society and Inequality*, Routledge, 2002

Schubert, Karsten, *The Curator's Egg: The Evolution of the Museum Concept from
   the French Revolution to the Present Day*, Ridinghouse, 2000

Serota, Nicholas, *Experience or Interpretation: the Dilemma of Museums of
   Modern Art*, Thames & Hudson, 2000

Smith, Rupert, *The Museum: Behind the Scenes at The British Museum*, BBC
   Books, 2007

Stourton, James, *Great Collectors of Our Time: Art Collecting Since 1945*, Scala,
   2007

Stourton, James, and Charles Sebag-Montefiore, *The British as Art Collectors:
   from the Tudors to the Present*, Scala, 2012

Thea, Carolee, *On Curating: Interviews with Ten International Curators*,
   New York: Art Publishers, 2009

Weil, Stephen, *Making Museums Matter*, Smithsonian Institution, 2002

Whitehead, Christopher, *Interpreting Art in Museums and Galleries*,
   Routledge, 2012

Wilson, David M., *The British Museum: Purpose and Politics*, British Museum
      Press, 1989

ARTICLES
Fraser, Andrea, 'A Museum Is not a Business: It Is Run in a Businesslike Fashion',
in Nina Möntmann (ed.), *Art and Its Institutions*, Black Dog Publishing, 2006,
pp 86–98
Huyssen, Andreas, 'Escape from Amnesia: The Museum as Mass Medium', in
Twilight Memories, Routledge, 1995, pp 13–36

Globalisation

Harvey, David, *Spaces of Global Capitalism: Towards a Theory of Uneven
      Geographical Development*, Verso, 2006
Steger, Manfred B., *Globalization: A Very Short Introduction*, Oxford University
      Press, 2003
Chua, Amy, *World on Fire: How Exporting Free Market Democracy Breeds Ethnic
      Hatred and Global Instability*, Anchor, 2004
Chantal Pontbriand, *The Contemporary, The Common: Art in a Globalizing
      World*, Sternberg Press, 2013
Lee, Pamela S., *Forgetting the Artworld*, MIT Press, 2012
Belting, Hans, Andrea Buddensieg and Peter Wiebel (eds), *The Global
      Contemporary and the Rise of New Art Worlds*, MIT Press, 2013

Photography

Hacking, Juliet, *Lives of the Great Photographers*, Thames & Hudson, 2015
Hacking, Juliet (ed.), *Photograph: The Whole Story*, Thames & Hudson, 2012

CONTRIBUTORS

David Bellingham

Dr David Bellingham is Programme Director for the Master's Degree in Art Business at Sotheby's Institute of Art, where he lectures on art world ethics and the market for antiquities and Old Masters. His research interests include issues of replication, authenticity and the symbiosis of public and commercial art sectors.

Jeffrey Boloten

Jeffrey Boloten is Co-Founder of ArtInsight Ltd, and Programme Leader for the Art & Business Semester Programme at Sotheby's Institute of Art, London. A member of the Advisory Board for the Photo Shanghai art fair, Jeffrey is also the author of 'The Market for Photography' article in the Grove *Dictionary of Art*, Oxford University Press.

Derrick Chong

Dr Derrick Chong is faculty in the School of Management at Royal Holloway, University of London. He co-edited *The Art Business* (2008, Routledge) with Iain Robertson and *Arts Management* (Routledge 2002; revised 2010; new edition in progress). He won the 2011 John Molson MBA International Case Writing Competition for addressing sponsorship between BP and Tate following the Gulf of Mexico catastrophe.

Tom Christopherson

Tom Christopherson is Head of Art and Law Studies at Sotheby's Institute of Art, London. He is a solicitor and formerly European General Counsel, Sotheby's. Tom was appointed Master of the Worshipful Company of Art Scholars in 2016.

Lis Darby

Dr Lis Darby joined Sotheby's Institute of Art in 1984. She is currently Programme Director, MA in Contemporary Design. Her publications include *The Cult of the Prince Consort* (1983) and essays on twentieth-century and contemporary design in *Understanding Art Objects: Thinking Through the Eye* (2009) and *Art and Authenticity* (2012). She is a committee member of the Decorative Arts Society.

Gareth Fletcher

Gareth Fletcher is a Lecturer in Art Business at Sotheby's Institute of Art. He is Co-Academic Leader of the Art Business, Foundations and Placement semester course and Art and Its Markets summer study programme. He has been awarded a TECHNE AHRC scholarship to pursue a PhD examining the semiotics of provenance information.

Melanie Gerlis

Melanie Gerlis became the art market columnist for the *Financial Times* in September 2016. She was previously Art Market Editor at *The Art Newspaper* (2007–16), prior to which she worked in financial communications (1996–2005). She has a BA from Cambridge University and an MA from Sotheby's Institute of Art. Her book *Art as an Investment?* was published in 2014 (Lund Humphries).

Jos Hackforth-Jones

Professor Jos Hackforth-Jones is Director of Sotheby's Institute of Art, London. She has published widely on art-historical subjects, including most recently *Art and Authenticity* (co-edited with Megan Aldrich, Lund Humphries, 2012). She is a Fellow of the Royal Society of Arts.

Yasmin Railton

Dr Yasmin Railton is a Lecturer in Art Business at Sotheby's Institute of Art, London. Her specialisms include modern/contemporary art, conservation and art market research. She has an MA from Sotheby's Institute of Art and a PhD from the Courtauld Institute.

Iain Robertson

Dr Iain Robertson is Head of Art Business Studies at Sotheby's Institute of Art and author of *Understanding Art Markets: Inside the World of Art and Business* (2016) and *A New Art from Emerging Markets* (2011). A forthcoming text, *New Art, New Markets*, will be published in 2017. He is a consultant to banks in Asia and Europe and visiting professor to universities in Portugal and China.

Marios Samdanis

Dr Marios Samdanis is a Lecturer in Art Business at Sotheby's Institute of Art, London. Marios obtained his PhD in Management from the University of Kent in 2015. Previously he taught at the University of London, and his research in creative industries has appeared in international journals and conferences.

INDEX

decorative art 18, 42, 60, 61, 67, 68, 78, 148, 158, 161

La Defence, Paris 55

Degas, Edgar 107

Delacroix, Eugène 56

Delhi 35, 86

Deloitte, Miami 189, 190, 192

Deng Xiaoping 82

Design Art 20, 74–81

Design Miami 75

DesignArt London (later Pavilion of Art and Design (PAD)) 20, 74, 76

Detroit Institute of Arts 45, 54

Devonshire family 149

Documenta 35

Dodd, Philip 198

Doha 57, 84

Doig, Peter 65

Doyle, Arthur Conan 93

Drewe, John 101–2, 110, 139

Dubai 57, 87

Duchamp, Marcel 175

due diligence 12, 21, 22, 23, 24, 40, 99, 111–12, 136–45, 151, 190, 191

Dulwich Park 113

Durand-Ruel, Paul 64–5

Düsseldorf 76

Düsseldorf School of Photography 72

Duveen, Joseph 94, 185

eBay 166, 168

Ecole Nationale Supérieure des Beaux-Arts, Paris 33

Eden, Sir William 131

Egerton, Francis, 3rd Duke of Bridgewater 186

Egerton, Francis Ronald, 7th Duke of Sutherland 186

Egypt 61, 82, 101

Electronic Superhighway: 2016-1966 exhibition, 2016, London 170

Elgin Marbles 43, 92

Ellis, Adrian 77

emerging markets 12, 13, 14, 19, 20, 24, 34, 35, 62, 67–8, 72, 82–9, 152–9, 160, 192

Engineering and Physical Sciences Research Council 100

Essers, Liza 196

Established and Sons, London 75, 79

Estella Collection 83

Estorick Collection 101

ethics 12, 21, 39–51, 62, 141, 199

Etsy 166

European Court of Justice 133

European Fine Art Fair (TEFAF) (formerly Pictura Art Fair), Maastricht 157, 158, 161, 166

European Union, 'InfoSoc Directive' (Directive 2001/19) 133, 266

exhibitions 16, 20, 26, 35, 61, 101, 103, 127, 130, 138, 150, 161, 168, 171, 175, 196, 198, 199

see also named exhibitions

Fake or Fortune (BBC programme) 25

fakes 12, 49, 50, 100, 101, 102, 110–11

Ffoulkes, Constance Jocelyn 93

Fine Art Fund 186, 191

Flavin, Dan 116

Foire Internationale d'Art Contemporain, Paris 160

Fondazione Sandretto Re Rebaudengo, Turin 198

Fontana, Lucio, *Concetto Spaziale, Attese* 161

Forbes' annual list 195

forgeries 12, 49, 50, 93, 94, 101, 108–10, 139–40

Foundation for Art and Creative Technologies (FACT), Liverpool 170

France 13, 25, 32, 54, 55, 64, 79, 128, 129, 130–1

see also named galleries, places etc.

François I, King of France 106

fraud 49, 101, 110

Freedberg, David 96

First published in 2016 by Lund Humphries in association with Sotheby's Institute of Art

Lund Humphries
Office 3, Book House
261A City Road
London
EC1V 1JX
UK

www.lundhumphries.com

Sotheby's Institute of Art	Sotheby's Institute of Art
30 Bedford Square	570 Lexington Avenue, 6th Floor
Bloomsbury	New York
London WC1B 3EE	NY 10022
UK	USA

© Jos Hackforth-Jones and Iain Robertson, 2016

British Library Cataloging in Publication Data. A catalogue record for this book is available from the British Library.

ISBN: 978-1-84822-091-1 (paperback)
ISBN: 978-1-84822-211-3 (ebk – PDF)
ISBN: 978-1-84822-212-0 (ebk – ePub)
ISBN: 978-1-84822-213-7 (ebk – mobi)

Set in Avenir and Garamond Premier
Printed in the United Kingdom